*Adventurous Spirit*

# Adventurous Spirit

# HEATHER HAWKINS

**MURDOCH BOOKS**

SYDNEY · LONDON

**Published in 2017 by Murdoch Books,**
**an imprint of Allen & Unwin**

Murdoch Books Australia
83 Alexander Street, Crows Nest NSW 2065
Phone: +61 (0)2 8425 0100
murdochbooks.com.au
info@murdochbooks.com.au

Murdoch Books UK
Ormond House, 26–27 Boswell Street, London WC1N 3JZ
Phone: +44 (0) 20 8785 5995
murdochbooks.co.uk
info@murdochbooks.co.uk

A cataloguing-in-publication entry is available from the catalogue of the National Library of Australia at nla.gov.au

ISBN  978 1 76052 280 3 Australia

*Front cover photographs* Doug Hawkins: Family photo and
   Mark Conlon: North Pole Marathon Photo
*Back cover photography* Douglas Frost
*Cover design* Vivien Valk
*Illustration* Amy McLean

Printed and bound in Australia by Griffin Press

10 9 8 7 6 5 4 3 2 1

The paper in this book is FSC® certified.
FSC® promotes environmentally responsible,
socially beneficial and economically viable
management of the world's forests.

# CONTENTS

# FOREWORD

## ROB DE CASTELLA AO MBE

Adventurous Spirt. What a wonderful name for this book ... and this remarkable woman. It defines who Heather Hawkins is, and her approach to life. It inspires us all to embrace (and even seek out) new, adventurous and sometimes frightening challenges of our own.

Heather's story provides us with an insight into the circumstances, beliefs and people in Heather's life, especially her father and early up bringing, that have culminated in creating this remarkable, energetic and unstoppable woman.

From Surf Lifesaving, Heather stumbled into distance running and found a passion. Running became so much more than a sport or health-related activity, it became a personal quest. Being inspired and inspiring, motivated to embrace challenges, and driven by the realisation that even in exhaustion, pain and complete fatigue that life is a gift that is only unwrapped through triumphing over tough goals.

Heather's core values and approach to life are what I want to see flourish in my own children, because it is only when we truly get outside our comfort zone that we find out who we really are, and grow to become stronger and more capable people. Outside our comfort zone is also where we make the greatest contribution to our loved ones and the community. It is where all the magic happens. But to do this we need an adventurous spirit.

*Adventurous Spirit* is told with an openness and sweetness that belies Heather's toughness; she is warm, caring and sensitive, while also being tough, ambitious and confident.

At a time of domestic and global uncertainty, and a void of great leaders, we must become our own leaders and be our own rocks. We can't always control what happens to us, but we can control how we respond to it, turning both the good and the bad into an opportunity to rise to a challenge and grow as individuals.

I really enjoyed reading this book and enthusiastically recommend it to everyone, because we all need to find our adventurous spirit, and have the confidence to let it soar.

*Rob de Castella AO MBE*
*Former Commonwealth Games and World Marathon Champion*
*Marathon World Record Holder 1981–1984*
*April 2017*

# INTRODUCTION

Sometimes our paths in life can take us in completely unexpected directions. It may even be our very own footsteps, and the dreams inside, that divert us away from our original plans. But whatever the reasons, and wherever we go, I say to you, gently and honestly, go ahead and embrace the change.

When I was a child I wished for a life that was happy and smooth—a reasonable wish for a shy, young heart. Yet as my life has unfolded, and the shade has at times overshadowed the light, I can honestly say that I am grateful. For today I am a wiser, deeper, stronger version of this 1960s child.

Challenges make us into challengers, whether they arrive by themselves, or if we put them there. They teach us to build resilience and positivity. Help us to discover who we are and that we can actually face up to things once thought way beyond our measure, and ultimately go a whole lot further than we originally think.

Inside each one of us dwells an adventurous spirit. It's true, it's there.

I'd caught subtle glimpses of mine growing up, and I'd seen it in my parents, but it wasn't until I was twenty-one years old that I really listened to its voice.

I'd love you to keep me company in the pages of this book. Stay awhile in the light and shade and soak up some colours of life. Stand with me on marathon start lines, climb majestic mountain passes, stare cancer in the face, race through the red desert dust until it plumes out way behind, and then settle in front of an outback sunset and marvel at its hues.

For then as the stars begin to dot the vast canopies above us, and the moon reaches out over the distant horizon, we can celebrate this incredible word that links us all so closely together—life!

*Prologue*

# THE GREAT HIMALAYA TRAIL

## *Amphu Labtsa Pass*

## 2016

The sound of my breathing is just as loud as the cracking and scraping of my crampons across the slippery rocks. This is intense, noisy work, and every step that I take, though it's measured and careful, is sending tiny shards of ice off to bounce and scatter into the Honku Basin far below.

Thankfully, there's no one down there, and thankfully I'm wearing a harness. I know I'm as safe as I can possibly be right now, hitched to the side of this impressive mountain in the far northeast of Nepal, because our Sherpas have set all these ropes.

Just ahead, Bek, Matt and Cal are tracking well. I can see their colourful backpacks climbing steadily. They move in single file, spaced apart, across a blue wavy layer of ice. Soon they're up onto another wall of grey, slippery rocks, their young legs are setting a cracking pace.

At my right shoulder is Tsering Lama, our expedition guide. He's my new-found friend and a highly experienced Sherpa with a megawatt smile. Tsering's in his element here, confident and nimble, and he's tasked with training and watching over us as we steadily learn the ropes. I don't need any convincing that I've definitely got the better end of the deal—he's got his work cut out for him, and I couldn't be in safer hands!

I slide my carabiner dutifully along the section of rope, all the way to the next anchor point and kneel in the snow to transfer myself onto the next vertical stage. Ice keeps tumbling away. What would normally be a fairly straightforward task is really difficult right now. I've got cold, fumbling fingers inside my thick gloves. I fiddle about with the frozen metal gadgets as deftly as I can.

'Safety first,' I mumble to myself as I secure the carabiner onto the next line. Then I say, 'Ascender second' as the climbing ascender goes onto there as well. These four little words help to keep me on track.

After what feels like an eternity, I'm safely past this anchor point and ready to go. I tell myself I'm 'getting faster and more adept'. I'm not sure if it's completely true, but it's my little positive self-talk to keep my spirits up.

I hoist myself up onto that daunting blue layer of ice. I can see that I'm only metres away from the high point of my day—it's a knife-edged pass called Amphu Labtsa that juts boldly into the sky at 5348 metres. It looks sensational. This is our crossing point, the safest way over a seemingly insurmountable jagged ridgeline that divides the Honku Basin from the Chukung Valley.

And hidden to our north, behind a cluster of other peaks and clouds are the legendary giants of Everest and Lhotse. I can feel their presence and I'm in awe. I get the very strong sense we're walking in their backyard, only passing through on their terms, and the very thought of being so close to them makes my heart beat a little bit faster.

Across the saddle of the pass, stretch long strings of prayer flags. They flap faithfully in the breeze. I imagine their prayers, peeling off one by one, wrapping themselves around our team, then flying off to protect other climbers on the higher, more distant peaks. It's a comforting thought, and behind my thermal buff I master a 'Tsering megawatt smile'.

So far we've kept a searing schedule. Amphu Labtsa is our third mountain pass in the space of three days. While it's certainly not the highest pass we've crossed (that title's taken by Sherpani Col at 6189 metres), it's by far the most challenging, with its intricate icy layers, rough slippery rocks and a steep gnarly gradient.

'Doing well, Ama!' I hear Tsering's voice in my ear. He's using my Nepalese name that the expedition team gave me, which means 'Mum', and that's kind of cool. I'm happy to be everyone's mum around here.

'Climb up here. There's a ledge to rest on while you wait your turn to go over the pass,' Tsering directs.

*That's an awesome idea*, I think to myself. I'm so relieved!

My fifty-two-kilogram frame has been carting around my ten-kilogram backpack for the past five hours, and teamed up with my bulky mountaineering harness, stash of chocolate bars, A4 size diary and heavy leather boots, it's no wonder I'm bordering on weary. I make it up onto the narrow rock ledge, breathless but happy, and sidle carefully across to my seat.

Right now, it's oxygen, not warmth that I need, so I pull my buff away from my face and lean back into the mountain to breathe. This altitude is truly testing my limits—it's so desperately airless up here. Despite being acclimatised to the point that I can function okay, when I'm climbing it becomes obvious that a lung-full of breath just doesn't deliver what it does back down at sea level.

I tell myself to slow my breathing down: 'In and out … In and out …' I count to ten … and try to focus. Above me tiny icicles drip off the rocks and make patterns on my sleeve. Finally my breathing slows and I become quiet.

The view from this temporary perch is absolutely amazing. Below my boots the Honku Basin stretches away to the east. It's so white and grey, and in its lap it cradles a series of snap-frozen lakes. I trace the origins of the meandering glaciers feeding down from the circling, jagged peaks.

In the distance, the mighty Makalu stands as a sentinel—it's the world's fifth highest mountain, and my favourite so far. It's been watching over us, while we've boulder-hopped around its base and slept beneath its shadow. I'll be sad to see it slip away from sight.

All around at eye level white, billowing clouds build on the background of immense blue sky. They remind me so much of the rolling waves in the Pacific Ocean back home.

'Am I really here?' I murmur to myself.

The very notion that a fifty-one-year-old suburban Sydney mum could be hanging off the side of a mountain in far-flung Nepal defies all logic. But it's true. I'm here, and I'm here with my children, and it's still early days into our five-month Himalayan trek. There's still so much adventure stretching out in front of us.

Cal is the first over the pass. He shakes hands with Lakpa, the Sherpa, and gives me an encouraging wave. He films us before quickly disappearing out of view. This leaves Bek, Matt and I to go.

I sit in the sun and wait my turn, and become lost in the immensity of the moment.

If I could write a letter to myself from this ledge, and deliver it back in time to the person that I was nine years ago, I would use words filled with hope and life. It would probably be several pages long, as I know I would ramble on with excitement and add lots of vivid descriptions about the trail and the people.

But then I would purposely sign it off with 'much love', and write in capitals at the very bottom of the page: 'THERE IS A SECOND CHANCE AT LIFE!' And this letter would then replace the other letter that I'd held in my hand at that time—the letter from Bondi Radiology with my scan results that said: 'Ovarian Cancer'.

These two words changed my world forever.

I could carry this new letter and read it over and over again—before my surgery, in the medical consults, during all those follow-up tests, and in the quiet times when I was alone. I would put it in my pocket to hold onto whenever I needed some extra light and hope. I'd share it with my husband and my kids, and we'd circle today's date on the calendar, and we'd dream of this epic adventure, of this high pass, and our future together as a family.

It's hard to believe here I am, right now, fulfilling this unexpected dream, attempting to do something I would have told you was completely impossible as I lay curled up in my hospital bed, simply longing to survive.

My thoughts are brought back to the present as the clouds are beginning to gather around Amphu Labtsa. Bek is near the top. So there's just Matt and I to go. I shuffle back across to the edge of the ledge and start climbing again. I reach another anchor point and get through this one quickly. 'I'm getting more adept,' I tell myself, and this time it's definitely true.

I'm now up on a long stretch of rope, across the ice, so I dig my crampons in at the toes and step up with momentum. It's a very ungainly gait, a bit like walking on the moon. I'm so glad there are only two more sections of rope to go, then I'm there (the pass that is, not the moon!).

In the next ten minutes or so I gain another 25 metres in altitude. I can feel the muscles in my arms and thighs beginning to shake with fatigue.

'You're doing really well, Ama! Love you!' Bek calls out from above.

I wave back and press on. This is such intense exercise. I take my hat off to every single person who's ever climbed Everest. That's another 3.5 kilometres up in the sky. I look up. I can't even imagine what it's like to climb that high!

Now it's Matt's turn at the top of the pass. 'The rope is clear! See you soon!' he calls out, and then disappears from sight down along the fixed lines into Chukung Valley.

'I'm up next!' I blurt out. I'm so elated. I turn to Tsering and smile. I feel like a child. My emotions are running clear and unedited. All I have in my head and heart right now is joy and the sheer determination to get to the top. I'm here and I'm totally in the moment.

After fifty-one years, it's finally taken these mountains to teach me to think like this, to live in the here and now, and I'll do my best to hold onto this simple, yet profound wisp of wisdom.

I count my steps and keep looking up. All around me are angular, balancing rocks coated in snow. Step twenty-three, twenty-four, twenty-five. The wind whips over the pass and into my face. It's incredibly cold, but exhilarating. Step twenty-nine, thirty, thirty-one. I sense the slackness in the rope disappear. I'm getting closer to the anchor at the top. Step thirty-five, thirty-six, thirty-seven.

*Hooray, I'm here! I'm actually here*, I think to myself.

Tsering arrives a few seconds later. 'Well done, Ama!' he says proudly.

'Thank you, Tsering,' I reply, giving him a spontaneous hug.

We stand together in silence and gaze out. All around us are mountains and valleys, as far as the eye can see. This is a vast, majestic world. I turn slowly in a circle, taking it all in. There are no villages or highways, no corner shops or cafés. No evidence of the human hand at all.

I'm witnessing planet earth in all its rawness and power. It's wild and mighty, a magnificent and humbling place. I have no words. I know my place and it's an absolute privilege to be standing here. I watch as a bearded vulture rises past on an updraught. It spirals and soars. It's free on the wind. I turn to take some photos, and then look back and it's gone.

The morning sun is still shining in Honku Basin, but in the Chukung Valley there's misty rain sweeping up to the pass. The day is beginning to change. I linger for a few more minutes among the prayer flags, and whisper a prayer. Then I say goodbye to Makalu. I know it's now time to go.

I connect my carabiner and descender to the new section of rope and begin to abseil down. This side of the pass is far steeper than the east. It's a mixed blessing—easier on my lungs, but harder on my legs and arms. I dig the toes of my crampons into the ice and lean away from the mountain.

It takes a whole load of trust and my entire cache of concentration to climb down.

There are snowy sections where I fly like a super hero, and slippery rock shelves where I falter. 'Where do I put my feet?' I sing out to Tsering. I'm looking at a particularly technical wall.

He climbs over in no time and coaches me across. His voice is calm, reassuring. He can see a way through. The rain is inching ever closer and the wind is chilling. I pull up my buff to protect my face. It's time to get down off this ridge.

Far below I can make out our porters with their loads on the glacier moraine wall. They'll be at camp very soon. Cal, Bek and Matt are making good time too. The wind carries their voices up as they call out, 'rope's clear'.

I give them a wave before turning to face the mountain again. As I ease the rope through my figure eight descender, it scrapes my gloves and the friction warms up my hands. This is an added bonus. I look down and choose my steps carefully. I've had no slips so far, and I plan to keep it that way!

The temperature starts to drop. I can feel the chill of the wind through my thermal leggings and protective overpants. My nose begins to run and my eyes fill with water. I spin my buff around on my face to find a warmer, drier section. I'm getting close to the point where the fixed lines end and I can walk again on my own.

Just one last section and I'll be there. I clatter and scrape across the rocks and count my steps ... twenty, twenty-one, twenty-two, then I say, 'Figure eight descender off. Safety off', and I've made it. I step out by myself onto the snow-covered shale.

Back up the towering pass, Lakpa is steadily gathering up the anchors and ropes and Tsering gives him a hand. They descend together like soldiers with ropes looped across their chests.

From here on the path is easy to follow. There are deep sunken footprints in the snow that lead down to the scree. Tsering catches up to me and moves to the front. 'Keep up with me, Ama,' he instructs.

So I do. I follow his footsteps, exactly. Within minutes of leaving the rope, the misty rain catches up with us. We pull on our hoods and press on. The snow crunches up against our boots and the wind whips against our sides, but I don't care, I'm feeling unbelievably happy. We've just climbed over Amphu Labtsa. It's not that we've conquered this pass, but instead, we've been allowed to stand on its shoulders.

That's what I love about the Himalayas and what I love about this trail. Nature welcomes us, but on its own terms—this is another little wisp of wisdom to carry away home with me.

Suddenly we're into a steeper, deeper, snowy section and without warning my right knee buckles. I'm halfway through a step and the teeth of my crampons hook into the side of my gaiter. I have no time to react. I stumble and slide and Tsering's quick to grab me.

'Ama.' He shakes his head in concern.

I don't know whether to laugh or cry. I'm shaken, but okay. I stand up and brush the snow off my jacket as Tsering moves closer to my right shoulder and attaches a short rope to my harness. We'll be hitched together for this last section of steep snow. I feel a bit foolish, but I'm incredibly grateful for his quick-thinking and reflexes.

As we reach the shale and the gentler gradient of the moraine wall, Tsering unhitches me. My thoughts turn to camp, and I wonder how I'm going to fit this day into my diary—it's been a truly epic one!

Then it dawns on me, and I think back to the 'letter to myself' idea. I *will* write my 'future self' a letter instead.

And I *will* use all those words filled with hope and life, just as I needed all those years ago. It *will* be several pages long, as I know that I *will* ramble on with excitement and add lots of vivid descriptions about the pass and the people and the mountains and the prayer flags.

Then I'll purposely sign it off with 'much love' and write in even larger capitals at the bottom of the page: 'THERE DEFINITELY IS A SECOND CHANCE AT LIFE!' And I'll fold up this letter and put it in my jacket pocket, so that everyday I can remind myself that no matter where this trail takes me—all the way to the western border of Nepal and on to my full measure of days—that I'll have faith and my family and my friends at my shoulder.

I'll let the tears well up, and they'll be tears of joy, washing away any fragments of fear, and I'll be safe in the knowledge that no matter where I am, or how hard life becomes, that there will always be a way through.

# Chapter One

# MY FAMILY'S ADVENTUROUS SPIRIT

## 1931-86

Mum, Elva Metzenthen, and Dad, Bob Ingamells, had grown up around the corner from each other in Surrey Hills, Melbourne. But because they'd attended different schools and churches, and socialised in separate circles, they didn't really know each other that well. In fact, Dad's impression of Mum had always been that she was far too good for him.

Dad grew up to become an adventurous young man who raced cars around the block, to skid sideways under the railway bridge, while Mum was the sensible, sporty one who taught Sunday school at the local Methodist church and played netball.

After high school, Mum studied to become an industrial chemist and worked at Holeproof, while Dad studied and worked hard to become a licensed plumber. But all through these years his 'adventurous spirit' kept bubbling away inside.

Dad had always been fascinated by the early Australian and Antarctic Explorers, and he had read widely about their expeditions. So in 1955, he set off for eighteen months to chase his own dream to drive around Australia. It was a long time before Highway One was completely sealed.

His sister, Rosie, joined him for a good part of the journey too. She'd just finished her nursing training, and together they navigated the continent in a Peugeot 202 'bread wagon' using a crinkled, old Shell road map to guide them. Rosie was great company—bright, energetic and unfazed by all the dust and the unpredictability of life on the unmade roads. They got bogged, had to change multiple flat tyres, and broke down a long way from anywhere, but they always managed to get through.

When they arrived in Alice Springs, Rosie nursed at the local hospital and Dad did some plumbing work on the John Flynn Memorial Church and out at Hermannsburg Mission. It was during this trip that he met the artist Albert Namatjira, and Dad was totally inspired by his paintings.

As their adventure unfolded, Dad developed an ear infection. Despite being treated with tinctures and antibiotics throughout their travels, it became alarmingly worse. So by the time he and Rosie arrived home in Melbourne in 1956, it had spread to his inner ear. Dad was immediately placed on a stronger regime of antibiotics, and these curbed the infection, for the time being.

On one occasion, Dad needed a partner for a friend's wedding, and he was at a loss as to who to ask, having only recently returned from his trip. So after all those years of dancing around the edges, Dad finally plucked up enough courage to ask Elva to join him as his date. However, when he asked her, she declined, stating she was far too busy. Dad was devastated. But fortunately Elva's parents had overheard their phone conversation and encouraged her to change her mind. She phoned Dad back and said 'yes'! They were both twenty-four years old.

They quickly fell in love, and in 1957, Dad proposed to Mum on St Kilda Pier with the lights of Melbourne sparkling brightly on Port Phillip Bay. However, their relationship was about to be tested. For despite further rounds of antibiotics, Dad's inner ear infection spread into his brain. It now became a life-threatening situation. He underwent emergency surgery and for several days it was touch and go as he fought for his life. My mum didn't leave his side, as she said there was no way she was going to give up on him, no way she was going to let him go.

Fortunately, Dad pulled through, but sadly he lost all hearing in that ear. All that was left was the sound of his beating heart. It was a huge adjustment for him, as well as for Mum. It disturbed his sleep and he went from being a confident young man in social settings, to being awkward and self-conscious. He missed the parts of so many conversations, and people misunderstood his silence; however, Mum always stood next to him, to give subtle prompts and help him get through. Mum and Dad made an awesome team.

On the 25 October 1958, they were married in Surrey Hills in Melbourne. As newlyweds, Dad worked hard to establish his successful business, 'R & E Ingamells Plumbing', and Mum set up their house, did their business accounts and became a full-time mum.

I was born at Box Hill Hospital in Melbourne, on the 3 April 1965. Back in those days my dad wasn't allowed to set foot in the labour ward, so after racing Mum to hospital, he was told to go home and wait for their phone call.

As the afternoon stretched into evening, Dad switched on the investigative ABC TV program, *Four Corners*, to distract himself. Still the phone didn't ring. He became anxious, thinking that perhaps he should call the hospital.

Then there was a knock on the front window of our house in Nunawading. It was Mum's obstetrician. He was on his way home from the hospital and thought he'd save himself a phone call, as he had some good news.

Dad opened the window to be told that he had a healthy baby girl and Mum was also doing well. Relief gave way to joy!

Now there were five of us. Mum, Dad, my oldest brother, Trevor, who'd been born on Christmas Day in 1960, and Ray, another December baby born in 1962.

They called me Heather Joy.

On my first birthday I was given a little yellow teddy bear from my grandparents. I called her Teddy Girl, which in later years I abbreviated to 'TG the Bear'. I took her everywhere with me, and still do, on every single journey I embark upon.

But adventure kept bubbling away within our family.

So in 1968, Mum and Dad decided to make a huge family change. They sold our house in Nunawading, organised passports and paperwork, and we immigrated to Canada. Trevor, Ray and I were seven, five and three.

We had no relatives there, nor did we know anyone. Dad and Mum clearly felt it was time for a change, to step away from the stress of running a burgeoning business and to see more of the world. Canada was similar to Australia, being part of the Commonwealth, but it was so much closer to the rest of the world and would make the perfect launching pad for travelling together as a family.

In May 1968, we packed our world into several travelling trunks and suitcases and set sail for Vancouver on the P&O ocean liner *Oriana*. We stopped briefly in New Zealand, Fiji, and Hawaii. Then in Los Angeles we visited Disneyland and met Goofy and Mickey Mouse. In San Francisco, we rode on trams up steep, steep streets.

Finally, on the 27 July 1968, we disembarked with our possessions in the city of Victoria on Vancouver Island, and started a whole new life.

We found a house to rent and Dad searched for plumbing work. Trevor and Ray started classes at the local school and I stayed with Mum before starting two days a week at preschool. On the weekends we explored the city and played in the local parks in among growing piles of golden maple leaves. Mum wrote letters home and Dad took photos to document our experience of living in a different country. These days were filled with wonder, yet also a little uncertainty as we adapted to making new friends, using a different currency, speaking with a Canadian accent, and finding our way along unfamiliar streets. Soon Dad found casual work and we settled ourselves into the rhythm of daily life.

Christmas arrived with its festive lights. They were absolutely beautiful.

It was our first Christmas away from home and we woke up early to find presents posted all the way from Australia. It was so exciting, for inside the wrapping paper were books and a football. However, they also brought a mix of emotions, particularly for Mum and Dad, for the handwritten cards reminded us of loved ones, so far away in the summer heat of Australia, absent from our dinner table and from our new life in the snow.

As 1969 arrived, the winter continued to be a whole lot colder than usual, meaning plumbing work for Dad became frustratingly inconsistent. It brought uncertainty and Mum and Dad began to wonder about our future in Canada.

Then news arrived from home that made their decision clearer. My mum's mum was starting to have problems with her lungs—side effects of radiotherapy she'd been receiving for treatment of breast cancer. It was time to start on our journey home.

Our planned route was to take us across the USA, to a ship sailing home from Montreal. Now, a road trip needs a car and a caravan, so we bought a dark blue Chevrolet and a dot of a van for our five-month journey. We wound down the massive windows and felt the wind in our faces and watched the country change around us.

Mum really looked the part in the passenger seat, with her cat-eye sunglasses and Dad bought himself a cowboy hat. Trevor and Ray busied themselves writing diaries and doing schoolwork by correspondence. I coloured in my notepads and daydreamed out the window. We collected cloth badges wherever we went, souvenirs, a snow dome or two, and we stayed for free at all the National Parks because we were international travellers.

We soon discovered that the USA was a vast, vast continent.

We explored beneath the towering trees of the Redwood forest, and squeezed our Chevrolet through the carved-out trunk of a gracious giant. We drove into Los Angeles and accidently found ourselves on the wrong side of the road. In Death Valley we searched for shade. Further down the road we held hands and stood in all four states at once: on the corner of Arizona, New Mexico, Colorado and Utah. We witnessed the depth and breadth of the Grand Canyon, and journeyed to Monument Valley, Bryce Canyon, Mesa Verde, and Yellowstone National Park.

One day, I left TG the Bear behind on a bench, but Dad turned around without hesitation and drove back to get her. We continued on to Oklahoma, New Orleans and across the expansive Mississippi River.

We arrived in Florida in hot, humid weather, and stayed in a caravan park dwarfed by a series of soaring sand dunes. After a lightning storm that night we found several zigzag strands of fulgurite—the silvery globs that occur when lightning strikes sand. But we had no idea as to how we could get them safely back to Australia.

We toured the Kennedy Space Centre at Cape Canaveral and gazed out at Apollo 11 as it sat waiting on Launchpad 39A, prior to its mission to the moon. More places flashed past our car windows: Washington DC, West Virginia, Blue Ridge Mountains and Pennsylvania. Then into New York City, where we joined the queues of tourists to explore Central Park, the Empire State Building, and to ride a ferry to the Statue of Liberty. We visited Niagra Falls and walked down into the tunnel behind the falls.

Then at last we were onto our final leg of the journey and pulled in to a little caravan park in Montreal. Over the next few days Mum and Dad took on the massive task of selling the car and caravan, and packing all our gear away into trunks and suitcases. Trevor, Ray and I helped as much as we could. Our next trip was to sail to England and embark on the P&O *Iberia* in London, to head back home.

Then the night before we sailed, I had to go and have an accident …

Near our caravan was a grassy hill, and Trevor, Ray and I ran to the top of it and rolled down. We did this a few times as dusk was falling. However, on my last roll down, I felt sharp pressure in my leg, and by the time I'd reached the bottom of the hill there was a large 10-centimetre jagged laceration at the top of my right thigh. It was bleeding profusely. Ray and Trevor carried me back to the caravan crying and desperately calling out to Mum and Dad. I can't begin to imagine how they must have felt.

Mum wrapped my leg up in clean white towels and the caravan park owner offered to drive us to the hospital to act as our interpreter—we couldn't speak French.

I remember so clearly waiting at the hospital, cradled in Mum's arms. It was a busy and noisy place, and Mum was understandably anxious. In the seat opposite me was a girl who'd fallen off her bike onto a gravel surface. She had terrible grazes on her hands, knees and face. I looked up at Mum and said, 'They need to see her first. She's very sad.'

But I was taken into the treatment room first. The nursing staff cleaned my wound. It was so painful and I wriggled and cried and generally exasperated them. Fifteen stitches later, they bandaged my little four-year-old leg and I was free to go with three lollipops—one for each of my brothers, and one for me.

Mum and Dad mentioned it several times over the years about how fortunate I'd been to not have any lasting injuries from that accident. But it wasn't until I started running in 2012, that it truly sank in. When I was teenager it was just an annoying, embarrassing scar, something that I'd consciously cover up with my hands whenever I was in my swimming cozzie. But today I've come to embrace it. It's significant. It shouts out about our adventure across North America and reminds me of how lucky I am to be able to run.

The next day I hobbled aboard the boat and we sailed to England. We travelled to Scotland and Eastern Europe briefly, and then on the 16 September 1969, we finally sailed for home. By now we were tall, skinny-legged children, who were very different to the ones who had left Australia almost two years ago.

Back in Melbourne, we moved into a grand, old weatherboard house called Rae Hill in Ringwood East. It belonged to some of Dad's relatives. I started school there, with a bag that was as big as me, and a crisp checked school uniform. Mum and Dad bought me a ginger kitten for my birthday and I promptly named her Muffy, after my teacher's cat.

Dad did some plumbing work but also trained and worked as a real estate agent. He came across a property that was for sale in Montrose. It was an old apple orchard, with a ramshackle farmhouse, which belied the property's glorious past.

Prior to being an orchard there'd been a guesthouse called Grande Vue on the top of the hill. For years guests would travel here in their vintage cars to experience the health benefits of breathing in the fresh country air and taking in the mountain views.

We moved in over the Christmas holidays of December 1970. Mum planted vegetables and daffodils, and Dad worked on improving the house. After a few months we had the luxury of an inside toilet.

My brothers and I went to Montrose Primary School. I started in year one. I can clearly remember the first day at school, meeting the principal, then after the bell had rung, being escorted with my brothers along the empty lino corridors to be introduced to our classes. As we walked I wished nervously that I could stay with them. I guess after all those months of travelling together, and the uncertainty of starting a new school, I was overwhelmed. Thankfully I soon settled in.

I loved school athletics day, because I could sprint. When I was in year six, a teacher entered me into an 800-metre race to earn some extra points for our House, Sturt—we needed just a few more to win. I'd already finished my earlier races and must have been on her radar, resting in the grass close by. I'd had no prior training for this distance, but I was willing to give two laps around the oval a go for extra points!

The starter's gun sounded and I started strongly. At first I was keeping up with the pack, but by the time the halfway mark arrived, I was tiring fast and dropping behind. This was a whole new experience. Suddenly I was out of my comfort zone, breathless and fatigued, and daunted by the distance. I trailed along on my concrete legs for another half a lap, before the sight of the finish line spurred me on.

'I have to earn some points for Sturt,' I said to myself and willed myself to pick up my pace.

One by one I moved up the field, and managed to cross the finish line in second place. As I slumped in the grass, trying to get my breath back, and feeling sick, there were two very clear thoughts in my head: *I am sure we've won the House competition ... and I am not cut out to be a long-distance runner!*

During these years, we had an old white station wagon and continued to head off on adventurous holidays with the caravan to Marysville for Easter. Then every Christmas we'd explore further afield, up into the remote high country beyond the Yarra Valley, and the along entire rugged coastline of Victoria, down to Tasmania, taking the car and caravan on the Empress of Tasmania, to the Flinders Ranges in South Australia, to New South Wales to see the Blue Mountains and Broken Hill. It was an eight-berth caravan and sometimes we'd take Grandma or Grandpa Ingamells with us too. I think that was the first time I'd ever seen false teeth in a glass!

Grandma Metzenthen passed away in 1971. Mum had been able to spend two extra precious years with her. We were considered to be a little too young to go to the funeral, so we went to school as usual that day. I don't recall seeing Mum cry very much. She must have kept her pain all to herself—that was the way she was, always doing her best to shield us from hurt, but it must have been so hard for her.

For many years my family attended church and that's where I learnt about having a faith.

In 1973, Dad designed and built his dream home, right where the original Grande Vue guesthouse had been at the top of our long, sloping paddocks. It was the perfect location for a house, with views out across the western face of Mount Dandenong, over to the Yarra Valley and far beyond to Mount Donna Buang jutting up in the Great Dividing Ranges.

Our house had floor to ceiling windows, long Oregon timber beams, and broad eaves designed to keep the summer sun out but let the winter sun in. These were designs that Dad had picked up from Canada and the USA. He even put in wooden shingles as feature walls in several rooms.

He put in a built-in wall unit with multiple shelves in the lounge room. It was on these shelves that Mum and Dad finally unpacked our treasures from our travels: the fulgurite from Florida, dolls in national dress, teaspoons, mugs, tiny wooden lifebuoys from the *Oriana* and *Iberia*, painted stone tools from the Navajo Indians, boomerangs from 1956, and photos of our family. I'd often pick things up on my way past and have a look at them.

In the cupboards below were albums of tiny black and white family photos. They were stuck to the pages with photo corners and captioned in scrawly handwriting from the 1940s. Next to them were tall stacks of yellow boxes containing Dad's 8500

Kodak slides. On their lids were place names such as Texas, Oklahoma, New York, and Death Valley. So many memories, and so many adventures tucked secretly away in there.

I went to Pembroke High, as a very shy, awkward teenager. I had short, brown, curly unremarkable hair, and I didn't wear the latest designer jeans, didn't wear makeup, and I was quiet in class and studied hard. I had some great friends who shared the full six years with me, along with some awesome teachers too.

But life has its light and shade and we had bullies at high school who'd tear confidence apart with their words and undo all that positivity from childhood. They called me ugly and uncool. I pretended to ignore them, and acted like it didn't hurt, but it did. I felt powerless, humiliated and so very far from perfect, and I'd get home from school and look in the mirror and wonder if I'd ever be beautiful.

Mum could always pick up pretty quickly whenever I was upset. She was intuitive and compassionate. I'd sob while she hugged me and she'd explain things in her gentle, wise way saying, 'It's sad that these girls are so cruel. Obviously they don't understand that people have different views, beliefs, looks … this is what makes this world a far richer, better place. Heather, I know this hurts so much right now, but you need to keep being you, don't change because of them. Hold onto the way you do things, the way you dress, who you are and don't be made to feel any less because of it. Remember you are beautiful on the outside and on the inside too.'

Mum helped me get through the hurt. It was a huge life lesson for me and has made me a whole lot more understanding and accepting of others, and mindful of my words. Words are powerful and they need to be used for good, for encourage-ment, and to always bring light and hope.

In the later years of high school, I got on with my studies, hung out with my friends and was happy. I remember a specific question for my creative writing essay on my HSC English Exam: 'If there's no place like home, then why leave?' *A perfect question*, I thought.

I wrote about my dad and about his yearning for adventure from a very young age. How he sprinkled our childhood with stories from his quest around Australia. About our life in Canada and travelling around the world, and our realisation—when we'd taken ourselves away to the furthest point from home, and we'd had our fill of adventure—that our original home, with all the people we loved, was actually the place where we wanted to be. I was so happy I got an 'A'.

With exams over, it was time to start a whole new stage in life. I started my studies to become a registered general nurse, in May 1983, at Box Hill Hospital—the hospital where I was born.

As a trainee nurse I lived in the nurses home and attended classes and worked on the wards. We had eight weeks of Preliminary Training School in the classroom, and then we were rostered onto the wards. My first shift was a busy morning shift from 7am to 3.15pm in the male Surgical Ward 2 South. I had six patients to care for, with fractured legs strung up in traction.

I learned very quickly about priorities, how to multi-task, to get everyone bathed, their beds made, and dressings changed on their wounds. As I pulled on my cape to sign off for the day, the sister in charge barked at me, 'Nurse Ingamells, you still have to write up their nursing notes up in their Patient History.'

I didn't know I had to do that. I left the ward well after 4pm, rattled and exhausted, but glad that I'd survived my first day.

I particularly loved my twelve-week stint in surgery, often working as an instrument nurse, because it was rewarding to see lives saved and changed.

In early 1986, towards the end of my nursing training, I started to think about travelling. Dad came with me to road test a number of campervans and got me a good deal. He was an awesome negotiator. I simply stood next to him, speechless and shaking in my shoes.

Following my graduation from nursing in May 1986, I planned a test trip for four weeks around country Victoria. Dad was incredibly excited for me. Mum was happy, but as equally worried that I was travelling alone.

Dad showed me how to change a tyre, to fill up the radiator, check the oil, and he gave me tips on driving and camping and told me the most important piece of travel advice I'd ever hear in my life—never drive after sunset in the outback. This was a very important lesson to learn.

The test trip in June went well. I adjusted quickly to the action of driving with a gearstick on the steering column, and worked out that I wasn't too lonely with my own company. In fact, I loved the easy rhythm and freedom of travelling every day.

I set off along the Great Ocean Road and drove west to Adelaide, and then I turned south to explore its peninsulas. The weeks flew by and before I knew it I was heading home from the Murray River in Mildura.

I came home with renewed confidence that I could now embark on a much longer trip. I felt ready to follow in the footsteps of my dad and to one day head off to outback Australia.

On one misty morning in July 1986, I hugged Mum and Dad goodbye and drove down our long gravel driveway.

I looked back in the rear-vision mirror until I couldn't see them anymore. But as torn as I was, and despite the tears that wouldn't stop flowing, I knew it was time ... time for my very first long adventure alone.

*Chapter Two*

# TWO JOB INTERVIEWS AND AN ADVENTUROUS DRIVE

## 1986

'Why don't you come in for a 10am interview tomorrow,' the matron suggested to me over the phone.

'Thank you, that would be lovely. I look forward to seeing you then,' I replied politely and hung up.

'Yes!' I shouted out loud, as the remaining coins came tumbling out of the payphone. I scooped them up, pushed open the glass door of the booth and walked off to the Alice Springs Post Office. There was a parcel waiting for me.

I was really hoping that there would be a nursing position available at Alice Springs Hospital. It didn't matter to me which ward—medical or surgical, children's or accident and emergency—I was just keen to get a job, and accommodation at the nurses home.

I was sure that I had enough experience. Fresh out of Box Hill Hospital in Melbourne, graduating in May, I had polished leather shoes, a red cape and a starched white uniform. I'd only left Melbourne six weeks ago in my campervan, leaving my world behind—my family, my friends, and a secure nursing job—trading it all in for a road trip. I couldn't really explain why, except that the pull inside me to go and explore was stronger than the anchor that held me at home.

The parcel at the post office was from Mum and Dad and contained a four-page-handwritten letter, a photo of Mum feeding kookaburras in our garden, and a book about the Royal Flying Doctor Service. It was little slice of love from home.

The next morning I put on my favourite floral dress and flat shoes. It was a dramatic change from the wardrobe I'd been wearing those past six weeks, of faded T-shirts, crumpled shorts and desert boots.

I gathered all my documentation together and put the papers and certificates within easy reach in the glove box, then drove off to my interview with the Matron. I was extremely nervous.

I followed the hospital corridors to the main office and within minutes I was sitting across from the matron at a large wooden desk. She was a strong, robust woman, with a practical, no fuss manner—the way all matrons seemed to be. Between us were piles of forms needing attention, a world of responsibility and a tiny little pot plant. Her assistant brought in a tray with a teapot, teacups and biscuits.

As she looked over my qualifications, I perched myself on the edge of my chair and politely sipped my tea.

'So, Sister Ingamells,' Matron said, picking up her teacup and cutting through my thoughts. 'Your qualifications look fine. You present well. I'm wondering when can you start? Tomorrow?'

I swallowed my tea. 'Tomorrow, yes, I can certainly start tomorrow.' I was very surprised and relieved. I couldn't believe she'd only asked me two questions.

'Well then, we'll assign you to Ward Five, one of the children's wards. Let me check the roster. I'll put you down for an early shift tomorrow, that way you can have orientation following the handover from nightshift. Now come with me and I'll point you in the direction of the pay office, and show you where you can collect your uniform and organise accommodation at the nurses home.'

So, that was me sorted, just like that. Now that my journey had brought me to Alice Springs, I was 'picking up the baton' that Dad had passed on to me, all the way back in 1956.

I couldn't wait to call him from that payphone!

I settled into Ward Five quickly. The other nursing staff were great. Many were travellers just like me. We cared for children, mainly toddlers, but there were some as young as eight weeks old. We treated them for gastroenteritis, conjunctivitis, chest and ear infections. Many of them were from remote Aboriginal communities, several hours drive away along the red dusty tracks, and because of this, their families stayed with them in the ward too. It was a fun, lively, busy place to work.

The weeks went by and August turned into September, which then turned into October. In that time I got around town on a bicycle, had picnics in the Gaps of the McDonnell Ranges, drove to Ormiston Gorge and Glenn Helen Gorge in my campervan, watched sunrises and sunsets from Anzac Hill, worked hard and made new friends.

And then in early October, I signed up to do a skydiving course at the old Alice Springs airport. It was outrageously exhilarating, but terrifying, doing three solo static line jumps.

It was during this month that I started to make enquiries to see if there was any work available as a governess on a cattle station. I thought it would be a really unique thing to do—living in the middle of nowhere, living on the land with a family and a few thousand head of cattle. But I was informed that there wasn't anything currently available, in fact jobs were very difficult to come by, and so I put that idea aside.

I decided to just keep working in Ward Five and wait to see what 1987 brought.

And I remember well a particular day that changed the whole course of my journey ...

After working eight straight days, I've clocked up four rostered days off, that's a mini holiday, so I decide to travel further afield to Uluru and Kata Tjuta National Park. It's only 460-kilometres southwest of Alice Springs. My plan is to work an early shift, pack my campervan and leave at 7am the next morning. But instead, I'm impatient, and as soon as I'm packed, I leave that afternoon.

I head south. On the Stuart Highway there's not much traffic at all, just the odd road train and a handful of caravans heading north. I pass Stuarts Well Roadhouse and Noel Fullerton's Camel Farm, and cross over a low concrete bridge spanning the empty riverbed of the Finke.

A sign to the Henbury Meteorite Craters and Kings Canyon appears on the right. It points to a rough, red track heading off at right angles. If only I was in a 4WD, I could turn here and take the back roads. The afternoon stretches on, as the bitumen stretches off to the horizon. The spinifex and saltbush scoot past either side.

Two and a half hours later, I pull in to the Erldunda Roadhouse. It's on the corner of the Stuart Highway and

Lasseter Highway, and it's my turn off to the west. A towering road train pulls in beside me. It's as big as a city block and the trailers hang a long way back from the bowsers.

I fill up with petrol and walk to the counter to pay and enquire about camping. As I wait to be served, I have this whole conversation in my head … *Do I really want to stay here? I could push on and get to Uluru tonight and have three full days there.*

I know I'll be breaking the golden rule of the outback— 'never drive after sunset because wildlife wander onto the road'. My dad's given me this piece of advice several times now. But I'll be okay, I'll drive carefully, and I'll put my high beam on.

So I pay for petrol, buy a sandwich and lemonade, and slip back behind my steering wheel. My indicator clicks methodically as I turn west onto the Lasseter Highway. Ahead on the horizon, the sun hides itself away. The sky glows a magnificent red, matching in perfectly with the sandhills. Up above, transient pink wispy clouds streak out across the sky. It's these majestic, intense colours of the outback that I love so much.

I flick my headlights on. Mount Ebenezer Roadhouse appears on the left, and then disappears. Beyond that, a radio tower pokes a red hole in the air. I have another two hours to go. I shift in my seat and nibble on the sandwich.

The Lasseter Highway curves around some sandhills then rises slightly. I press my dusty desert boot down on the accelerator and race to the top of the rise.

I catch a glimpse of a white saltpan to the north. Soon the last hint of daylight slips away and the night picks up where it left off and hangs the stars back up in the sky.

I flip on my high beams and slow my speed to 80 kilometres an hour. Then to 60 … I concentrate hard, and keep an eye out for any movement on the edge of my headlights. This feels so slow, but I don't want any issues. I drive up over another sandhill rise, around a slight bend … and then … drive straight into trouble!

Stretching out across the bitumen is a large herd of Angus cattle. They don't scatter, but instead stand dazzled and frozen in my headlights.

I slam on my brakes as hard as I can. But there is nowhere to go. I have no escape route. My tyres scream. My cassette player flies off the seat and into the dashboard. I grip the steering wheel with whitening knuckles … I keep pressing the brake to the floor … *come on, stop* … and then …

*Bang!*

I hit a steer and veer off towards the wall of sand on the side of the road. My seatbelt locks up and grabs me roughly around my chest. It takes my breath away, but it saves my life.

The impact shatters the windscreen and buckles the front left-hand side of my van. The bullbar twists and turns, taking out the left headlight as it goes. The passenger door flies open and the window disappears with a pop. Inside my cabin the dashboard caves in, all the way to where my cassette player had played, and shifts the steering wheel right up to my hip.

The momentum keeps ploughing me further into the red sand and clumps of spinifex, until I finally come to a stop. Then after all the deafening noise, there's absolute silence. I'm in shock. Shattered. Covered in shards of glass and blood and cow manure.

*What have I done?*

I take the keys out of the ignition, push open my door and wriggle my legs out from under the steering wheel. Apart from chest and abdominal bruising from the seatbelt, and a slightly cut knee, that's the extent of my injuries.

The same can't be said about the steer. Unfortunately he's no longer alive. The rest of his herd mill around in the sand dunes, and stare at me unhappily, before moving north into the night.

I sit myself down on the sandhill and look back at my van. The right headlight glows back at me feebly. I'm absolutely gutted. *I can't believe this.* My ticket to see the world, my campervan, is a mangled mess that looks like it just dropped out of the sky. I have no one else to blame but myself. *How am I going to tell Dad?*

But that's the least of my worries. I have a more immediate problem. *How am I going to get out of this predicament?* I look out along the road. No headlights glowing in either direction. *Who would be driving at this time of night anyway?* I simply have to sit and wait. Up above the stars are brilliant and beautiful. The Milky Way is a spectacular speckled sheet and the Southern Cross shines, familiar and strong.

Then some lights appear on the westerly horizon. I stand up. They track closer and closer. Soon I can hear the sound of an engine and headlights light the sky like a rare summer thunderstorm. Everything becomes unbearably bright.

I stand and wave frantically on the side of the road. It's a small ute with two people from a cattle station down south. They look at me, and my van, and shake their heads in disbelief. 'Are you okay?' they ask.

'Yes, I am,' I say, so relieved.

'Well, the only thing we can do for you is go and let the Severins know that you're here. You're on their property. This is their steer. Maybe they can give you a tow back to Curtin Springs Station tonight.'

'Thank you, that would be great,' I reply.

They do a U-turn and head back west. Within no time at all, their red tail-lights have slipped away into the night. The highway is quiet and dark again.

An hour later headlights appear from the west. This time it's a sturdy, dusty, Toyota 4WD that pulls up. They stop across the road from me and leave two tyres on the bitumen and their headlights on.

A tall, muscly man in a shirt with cut-off sleeves steps out of the cabin. With him is a young, blond-haired boy.

'Hi, I'm Heather,' I introduce myself.

'Hi, I'm Ashley, and this is my son, Ben. We're from Curtin Springs Station. Looks like you've had a bit of an accident. What were you doing driving at this time of night anyway?'

I explain what's happened, and my foolish decision not to stop at Erldunda, and Ashley listens intently with his hands on his hips.

I point back down the road to the steer laying there crumpled on the edge of their headlights. Ashley walks over to it and checks its branding. It's one of their stock.

*Oh dear ...*

He wanders back—he has a plan. 'Just give me few minutes,' he says evenly to Ben and I. 'I'll load the carcass onto the back of the 4WD and then we'll sort out your van.'

Ashley starts the engine and drives over to the steer. He manoeuvres the 4WD back and forwards until it straddles the road and the steer is positioned behind it. The headlights light up the spinifex grass on the sandhills. They make crazy sharp shadows. Ben and I walk down to help. I need to make myself useful.

With the carcass loaded, we turn our attention to my van.

'I guess you have two options, Heather. Either leave it here or attempt to tow it back to Curtin Springs tonight.'

'Is it possible to tow it back?' I ask hopefully.

'Well, we'll need to dig it out at the front, check that the left-hand tyre is okay, and attach a tow rope. Do you think

33

you'll be alright getting back behind the wheel to steer?' Ashley asks.

'I think so … I'll give it go, as long as there are no more cows on the road,' I joke, lamely.

'Hope not, we already have plenty of steak for breakfast,' Ashley quips.

I laugh with embarrassment. Ben grabs a shovel from the 4WD and we dig.

We take it in turns, passing the shovel like a relay baton. Gradually we shift the sand from the van.

The left front tyre has a deep groove in its tread, as it's been cut by the mangled wheel rim, but fortunately it is still inflated. Ashley locates the towing hook on the chassis.

He secures the rope and picks up the shovel on his way back to the 4WD.

'You two go over to the other side of the road while I do this.' He jumps back into the cabin. The engine roars. He leans out the side window and looks back over his elbow.

We cross the bitumen and Ben and I stand on the sandhill. The sound of twisting metal and breaking glass is horrible. The windscreen falls out and gets stuck behind the bullbar.

The tension in the tow rope steadily builds. The 4WD shudders but holds its ground. It's a tug of war. Something has to give …

I hold my breath and cross my fingers.

Seconds later the van begins to move. Sand spills away to the sides and the van limps its way back onto the bitumen.

I squeeze in behind my steering wheel. It's going to be tricky to steer, but I'll do my best.

Ashley closes my door as I do up my seatbelt. He leans in the open window to give me instructions. 'Now, there's a very real risk the van will veer off to the left. If things get too dangerous,' he cautions, 'we'll leave it. No heroics. Understood?'

'Yes.'

'Now hold on firmly. Leave your foot off the pedals and make sure your handbrake is off.'

'Okay,' I answer, trying to take it all in.

Ashley walks halfway back to his 4WD and turns back. 'Oh, and you'd better put your sunglasses on.'

'What?' That's a really weird thing to say at this hour of the night.

'Yeah, sunglasses. Not to look good, but there'll be bits of glass flying off that broken windscreen of yours.'

'Oh, okay, I see.'

I prise open the glove box as far as I can, find my sunglasses inside and slide them on.

'I must look pretty silly!' I laugh and shake my head.

'Okay then?' Ashley calls out.

I give him the thumbs up. And with that, he climbs into the ute.

We drive about 35 kilometres an hour. We don't pass anyone else on the journey, and I'm so glad that there are no more cattle to be seen. I concentrate hard.

We are getting there …

Ten minutes later our tyres cross a cattle grid. *Vrrrmp, vrrrmp.* It's a wonderful noise. Off to the right I can see the lights of the Curtin Springs Cattle Station. It looks like a castle. Lights shine out from the roadside store at the front and onto the trees and petrol pumps.

We head around the back, our vehicles rattling and jostling in the dirt. Not far to go now—only 30 metres or so. Ashley swings in near the homestead generator and garage and turns his engine off. My van drifts in to a stop. I fumble with my door handle and jump down and grab a bag of clothes from the back.

'Heather, I'll show you where you can sleep tonight and where the bathroom is to get cleaned up,' Ashley explains as we walk towards the homestead. 'Then, as soon as you're settled, I'll turn the generator off. We can talk things through in the morning.'

I'm so tired I operate on autopilot. I have the world's quickest shower and brush my teeth. I curl up in bed and pull the woollen blankets way up over my shoulders and burrow down. It's really cold. The generator hums for a couple more minutes out the back of the homestead, then everything goes silent and dark.

I try my very best to drift off to sleep … I'm relieved that I'm safe, and that my van has been retrieved, but I'm really anxious about what will happen tomorrow, and especially what my dad will say!

Morning arrives all too fast as the station generator roars to life. Out the window the sky is a faded denim blue and the sandhills a hazy wobble in the distance. I get up and head into the kitchen for breakfast. On the grill are several sizzling steaks.

'Would you like one of these? They're fresh,' Ashley asks.

I smile and get what he means, and get that he's joking. 'No, thanks, I'll just have some vegemite on toast, if that's okay,' I reply, grateful to be so well looked after.

'Of course, help yourself.' He passes me the bread.

I put some bread in the toaster and sit down next to Ben. He has his dinosaur figurines all lined up on the table.

'I checked out your van this morning,' Ashley says, turning his steak. 'You were lucky to get away with just a few cuts and bruises. That steering column should have crushed both your legs.'

'Yes, my guardian angel's been working overtime!' I reply.

Peter, Ashley's father, opens the screen door and walks in. 'Well hello, you're Heather. Welcome to Curtin Springs.' He shakes my hand and sits down opposite me.

Ashley makes him a cup of tea.

'So you're the one who hit the steer.'

'Yes, that's me. I'm really sorry, please let me know how much I owe you for that.'

'Okay. We'll think about it and let you know,' Peter says, before continuing, 'if you need to make any calls, please do. The phone is just in my office through there.'

'Thanks,' I reply. 'I'd love to speak with my mum and dad, and the hospital.'

'The hospital? You're alright, aren't you?'

'Yes, I'm fine. I just might need to change my next shift, just in case I'm not back in Alice Springs in four days.'

'Work? But I thought you were on holidays?' Ashley said.

'Well sort of … it's a working holiday. I work in Ward Five at the hospital in Alice. I'm a nurse.'

'How long've you been working there, Heather?' Peter asks.

'Two months. My plan is to stay for a few more months, then keep travelling north. But I guess that all depends now on the van. If it can't be fixed, then I'm not sure what I'll do.'

'Ever thought about doing something different?' Ashley asks.

'Yes, I have—'

The phone rings, and our conversation is left at that.

After breakfast, I wash my clothes from last night and hang them on the clothesline in the backyard. They'll be dry in a few minutes, as it's that hot. Then I head into the study to phone my mum and dad. I dial home anxiously.

They're shocked and concerned, but not angry. I'm so relieved! I really feel like I've let them down. I reassure them

I'm not injured and that I'm in good hands here, and Ashley, Peter and I will work out about the steer and find a way to get my van and me back to Alice Springs.

Dad offers to fly up, but I reassure him I'm okay. I finish the phone call in tears. I really love my parents, and the accident has reminded me of how precious life is and how quickly it could've all been taken away.

At 'smoko', Ashley, Peter and I work out that my campervan can be transported back to Alice Springs on the Great Northern road train. It delivers produce to Yulara a couple of times a week and is normally empty on its return run. I can catch a lift back with it too. It's a perfect plan. It will be coming past tomorrow night, so we just need to tow my van to the cattle ramp ready for loading.

Ben takes me around the homestead and shows me inside his classroom where he has his lessons for School of the Air. A two-way radio sits on the corner desk, with open books and a mailbag for his finished work to be delivered back to Alice Springs on the bus.

Ashley and Peter introduce me to the staff and show me the roadhouse. Several tourists are arriving with their caravans to fill up with petrol and to get photos underneath the iconic Curtin Springs sign. Off in the distance Mount Conner stands with a hazy blue tablecloth.

'Want to come on a bore run with Ben and I?' Peter asks me.

'Sure, that would be great,' I reply.

We hop into the 4WD that had towed my van last night and head north from the homestead. We rattle along the rutted tyre tracks and weave around desert oaks and donut-shaped clumps of spiky yellow spinifex. A long plume of red dust kicks up behind our tailgate.

The water bore has only recently been sunk and a new tank has been erected here. Peter wants to check that it's working well and that the tank is filling up. Twenty minutes later we see the circular blades of the windmill towering above the landscape. We bounce along and pull up at its base. I hop out of the 4WD and gaze up.

Above our heads the Comet Windmill creaks and groans. It's a remarkable piece of machinery. The six-foot blades turn steadily in the breeze as the clear, cool water gushes up from the earth and into the iron water tank and drinking troughs, where it brims and glistens. Shadows from the blades spin across pockets of hoof marks in the dried red mud.

I ask Peter lots of questions about the station. I'm fascinated by his personal story. He arrived here in 1956 with his wife, Dawn. It seems so remote today, but what must it have been like back then? Like living on the moon?

Back at the homestead we have lunch outside under the bough shed. Steak and salad is on the menu. In the afternoon I help Ben with some homework and hang out with his dog, Patch, and walk to the top of a sand dune near the cattle yards to watch the sunset. Ben brings his dinosaurs with him. It's another beautiful red sky.

Ashley then asks me a question, 'Heather, what would you say if I offered you the position of governess here next year for Ben? I think you'd be perfect for the job.'

I open my mouth to answer, but Ashley continues on.

'Now you don't have to give me an answer straight away. I'm aware that you've only known us for one day, well not even that, so take your time, think it over and let me know before you go tomorrow.'

'I don't need to. I'd love to do it.'

'Really?' Ashley sounds so surprised.

'Yes, really.'

'You're sure? What about your nursing? What about your travelling?'

'I can always go back to that, and there's plenty more time to explore Australia. The funny thing is that last week I actually enquired about work as a governess, but there was nothing available. This is perfect, and I'd love to do it.' I burst out laughing. *This has been the craziest twenty-four hours of my life.*

I sleep so much better tonight and wake up to the hum of the generator at 6am. I have vegemite on toast again for breakfast and spend the day helping out around the homestead, and in the roadhouse, watching tourists come and go with their caravans.

After dinner we wait near the cattle yards. It's 9pm. The Great Northern road train eases to a stop in front of us. Its air brakes hiss. It's an enormous blue and white truck, the size of a house, and the lights on top make it look like a magnificent travelling circus.

My campervan sits feebly on the old cattle ramp near the cattle yards ready to go. The road train backs into position and swings open its doors. With a nudge from the bullbar of his 4WD, Ashley pushes my van gently into the back of the truck.

*I'm ready to go.*

I turn to Ben and shake his hand. 'We'll have fun doing schoolwork together, I promise.'

I turn to Ashley and Peter and shake their hands too. 'Thank you so much for looking after me. And thanks for the job. I'll see you in January next year!'

So with that, I climb up into the passenger side of the road train. The engine whines and roars and we head east along the Lasseter Highway. It's a beast of a vehicle and I feel safe and sound in here.

Our headlights cut two huge chunks out of the night. It's 10pm and we drive back towards Alice Springs. Even though I'm really tired, I'm excited—I can't wait to be driving back here into a new unexpected chapter of my life.

*Chapter Three*

# ADVENTURES AT CURTIN SPRINGS STATION AS A GOVERNESS

## 1987

It's January 1987, and I'm heading back to Central Australia to start my year as a governess at Curtin Springs Cattle Station. My Uncle Bryson is with me, keeping me company on the long outback drive. He starts to read *Robinson Crusoe* to me as I pull away from the kerb. Little do I know this novel will thread together our journey, all the way along the Oodnadatta Track, to Alice Springs.

As sad as I am to say goodbye to family and friends, I'm filled with armloads of anticipation about what lies ahead—ten months working as a governess on Curtin Springs Cattle Station, a property that's 100 kilometres long and 40 kilometres wide, in the grip of drought and 2256 kilometres from home.

We head northwest across Victoria and up into the Flinders Ranges in South Australia. It takes us a couple of days. I quickly add Wilpena Pound to my list of favourite places because of all the magnificent rock formations and the gum trees.

From here we drive to Hawker and on to Marree, the official start of the Oodnadatta Track. There's a deserted railway siding in the heart of town where the Old Ghan train used to pull in, bringing crowds and supplies. Today it's empty, disused, and the life-giving engine and carriages are gone. There's a profound sense of loss in this place.

We fill up with petrol and water and leave early the next day to rattle out along the red gibber plains. Now our serious driving begins ...

I concentrate hard as the morning sun beats down, and dust and small stones trip up behind us. There's no button for air conditioning on our dashboard, so our windows are wound all the way down. The hot desert air gusts in. It's not long before I'm covered in dried sweat and grit, and my hands alternate between slipping off and sticking to the steering wheel.

Today, I tell myself, it will just be a matter of driving on, drinking from my water bottle and handling it all. I glance at the odometer, it's racing around, and I'm keenly aware every kilometre that I drive right now is taking me further away from the world where I grew up. From the little town of Montrose nestled in the foothills of the Dandenong Ranges, with its drenching winter rains and blue rhododendron gardens. Further away from my brothers and Mum and Dad, and my friends from nursing, church and school.

Everyone there is getting on with their lives, pursuing their careers, remaining connected. But I'm not. I'm out of touch ... and I've put myself here ... *Why?*

All I know is that this desire to travel and explore is running so deep right now that it's pulling me away. Instead of signing up for a staffing year as a fresh graduate nurse at Box Hill Hospital, here I am, out on this track, trusting instincts and chasing dreams. I tell myself I'm not throwing my life away, or wasting opportunities. I'm simply giving myself the best chance to be free, to explore this country, create my own opportunities … to be me.

Not too far north we stop for a break and look out across Lake Eyre. It's so vast and white, with not a hint of water. It's been slowly baked dry in a very hot oven, and then generously seasoned with salt.

Bryson reads out loud from chapter three. The kilometres melt away in the 36 °C heat, and Robinson Crusoe is captured by pirates but manages to escape—my speed correlates to what's going on in the book!

We pull into the pub at William Creek, hot, thirsty and with my forearms feeling shattered from steering on the rough road. I order two cold soft drinks from the character behind the bar. All around us the walls are papered with hundreds of business cards pinned there by dusty travellers just like us. Maybe my dad's business card is here from his travels with my brother Trevor to the Simpson Desert four years ago. He'd told me about this pub. I sip my drink and study the wall, moving methodically up and down …

Then I find it, to the left of the bar, a light blue business card with 'R & E Ingamells Plumbing' in bold black print!

'Hey, Bryson, here it is!' I call out.

Bryson wanders over to look. 'Well, well,' he says.

I tear a piece of paper out of my diary, shape it into a little rectangle, and write: 'Heather Ingamells—Plumber's daughter' and pin it right next to Dad's. *Perfect!*

That night we camp a little further north near a dry riverbed and a rusting railway bridge. It's a beautiful sunset. We set up our tents as the cool desert air settles in. I rug up in my old green knitted jumper. Bryson reads chapter four and five by lamplight, and I listen and look up at the stars. Robinson Crusoe is shipwrecked and becomes stranded on the desert island.

In the morning our 4WD won't start. It has a flat battery. I can't believe it. We're stranded! *What are we going to do?* We're parked off the road in a dip, so there's no way we can push start it from here.

Fortunately, this 1978 model Toyota Landcruiser has a hand crank start handle, and thankfully Bryson remembers how to use this, because I really don't have a clue. We take turns, turning it around. It reminds me of the old vintage cars in Hollywood movies and I wonder if it will really work. Eventually the engine fires up and we get back on the road—we're rescued from our own desert island!

The Stuart Range appears up north and the track twists and turns with a number of sharp bends, so I have to keep my wits about me. Bryson closes his book and 'drives' with me. Without warning I hit a wash away and the 4WD bounces wildly. My guitar, which has been sitting on my bags in the back, hits the roof and crashes back down again. It's a sickening sound and I hope it's going to be okay.

Soon we find ourselves at Oodnadatta. I pull in to the roadhouse and instead of business cards pinned to the wall, it's painted completely in pink. There's another character behind the counter. It's a great opportunity to stretch our legs, check my guitar, and for Bryson to rest his eyes from chapter eight.

We camp here for the night and fortunately the battery of our 4WD has recharged from yesterday's drive, so the engine fires up the next morning.

Today the Oodnadatta Track is flat and straight, and I relax a whole lot more behind the wheel. A short way out of town the Old Ghan railway line and the Overland Telegraph Line head off north while the track veers west to Marla Bore. We've got 200 kilometres to go. Soon we'll be back onto the bitumen of the Stuart Highway and back among the other travellers and road trains.

Bryson reads on and by the time we reach Marla, he's finishing chapter fourteen. Robinson Crusoe has discovered he's not alone on the island and neither are we, as it's a busy campground here.

The next day we drive all the way to Alice Springs. It's blisteringly hot. We stop at Erldunda, the site of the infamous turn-off that I'd made three months ago. Then on past the sign to Henbury Meteorite Craters and Kings Canyon, over the Finke riverbed, past the Camel Farm and on through chapter twenty of *Robinson Crusoe*. Bryson's reading fast, but we arrive mid-afternoon, a little too soon for him to finish the book.

The next morning we stop off to pick Ben up from his relative's place, and I say a tearful farewell to Uncle Bryson. He's been great company and it's been a unique journey. He'll be flying back to Melbourne in a few days. I'll have to read those remaining chapters another time. Bryson reassures me that Robinson Crusoe does make it off the desert island and moves on with his life … and I guess we do too, as we say our goodbyes and head off into brand-new chapters of our lives.

Soon Ben and I are back on the Stuart Highway, chasing unattainable heat shimmers. We turn right onto the Lasseter Highway and drive past the spot where I hit the steer all those months ago. I point it out to Ben. Everything looks so normal in bright daylight, except for that obvious hole where my van wedged itself in the sand dune!

The first of many signs appear on the left. 'Curtin Springs—petrol and cool drinks'. My heart races faster. I have so much to look forward to—getting to know Ben's family better, taking up a role on a working cattle station, learning the ropes and getting involved, and gaining some earthy, practical wisdom. This experience I'm sure, will make me a stronger person—more resilient and resourceful, less shy and more confident.

I'm counting on it to help clarify who I am and what I want to do with my life from here. I don't kid myself that it's going to be easy or enjoyable all the time. I know I'll get tired, homesick, and I'll have lonely days when I'll question what I'm doing out here. But maybe, just maybe, when I feel that way, I can pour myself into doing creative things, like writing a journal, writing songs, writing letters home, and that will help this city girl flourish in this harsh, dusty, remote, outback environment.

A little while later we rattle across the cattle grid and pull in to the back of Curtin Springs homestead. I ease down from the driver's seat and stretch. My creased, sweaty shorts are stuck firmly to the back of my legs.

Patch, Ben's dog, comes barking and racing out across the yard. He kicks up a cloud of dust as he spins around our legs with joy. I put my hands on my hips and look around, refamiliarising myself with the sandstone homestead, and the water tank and the cacti in the garden bed. *Wow! This is my home for the next ten months.* What a thought!

Peter walks over and welcomes us back warmly. 'Come in to the kitchen for a cup of tea,' he insists.

*That's a fantastic idea!*

Later, Ben and I unpack the 4WD and lug our gear in through the flyscreen door. Ben points me to my bedroom, and drags his bag into his. Mine is the spare room with fresh wallpaper, a wooden wardrobe and a window into the sunroom. The sheets are crisp from a day out flapping on the clothesline, and a woollen blanket sits in neat folds at the foot of the bed. I lay my backpack down and lean my guitar up against the wall.

'I didn't know you played the guitar! It's a really nice one,' Ben says, reappearing in my doorway.

I look over at my guitar. It is a beautiful one made from yellow varnished wood with an intricate pattern around the sound hole on the front.

'My Aunty Christine gave it to me when I was thirteen. It's an old Spanish one. Mind you, I should have bought a guitar case to protect it before I started travelling. Take a look at this.' I turn the guitar on its side and run my finger along a hairline crack in the case. 'That's from me hitting a pothole on the Oodnadatta Track. I have a habit of hitting things when I drive, don't I! Cows … potholes …'

Ben laughs and shakes his head, then asks, 'What kind of songs do you play?'

'A few like "Country Road", "Blowing in the Wind", "Kumbaya", and some of my own.'

He shakes his head, he hasn't heard of any of them.

I put the guitar on my knee, make a chord with my left hand on the strut and strum the nylon strings. The guitar comes to life, but it's a little out of tune, that crack is twisting the case and loosening the strings.

At afternoon smoko, I catch up with the other cattle station staff. Ashley is away overseas on a scholarship, but there's other familiar faces. I shake their hands as Peter introduces me.

'So this is Kiwi, our carpenter, the handyman.'

'Hi Kiwi, good to meet you.'

'Well hello, Heather, don't you talk like the queen!'

I'm so embarrassed. I blush. *Surely he's joking?* I know I grew up in Melbourne, but I don't think I sound posh.

The afternoon is spent unpacking my world and washing a bagful of sweaty, dusty clothes. I wander out to the clothesline and by the time I've pegged the last sock up, the first one is completely dry.

The homestead generator hums on as a gentle soothing dusk settles across the sky. I tumble into bed at 10pm, curl up and pull the thick woollen blankets up around my shoulders to block out the cold. Tomorrow, Ben and I will get the classroom organised and prepare for the school year ahead.

I close my eyes and drift off to sleep ... *I still can't believe that I'm here.*

The next morning we grab a bucket, a broom and a fistful of cleaning cloths. We have a job to do. The classroom is a demountable building that's been sitting idle for a couple of months, so while I sweep and dust and squeal at spider webs, Ben giggles and washes the windows.

There's a laminated kitchen bench where the School of the Air two-way radio sits, and two desks, Ben's and mine. We stick posters up on the wall, one of a tiger behind Ben's chair, and next to a world globe on my desk, I put a tiny pot with a little cactus and an empty vegemite jar filled with coloured pencils and pens.

Peter comes in to check the radio and gets it working. We'll be ready for the School Assembly over the air tomorrow, and following that, for Ben's year four class with Mrs Simms.

After lunch we put on our hats and take Patch to explore the cattle yards and beyond. We head to the western end of the airstrip, and after some coaxing from Ben, we all run along the runway.

As we near the halfway mark, I ask Ben, 'Will your teacher, Mrs Simms, fly in to visit you in the next few months?'

Ben nods, but keeps looking at the ground. It's hard to gauge if he's keen about the idea or not.

So I ask him another question, 'Have you ever flown in a small plane?'

'Yes, in the mail plane last year. We played "spot the cattle" and our homestead looked so small. I got a great view of Mount Conner too,' Ben answers with a whole lot more enthusiasm and points south to where Mount Conner rises up as a striking sandstone, table-topped mountain. Sloping scree spills down it's northern face.

'We'll climb that when the weather gets cooler,' I promise.

After afternoon smoko, I take an extra mug of tea to the classroom and spend some time looking over the school lessons for the coming week. I look around the walls and ceiling. We'll fill this place with colour and mobiles and art, and by the end of the year there won't be a spare centimetre of wall—just like William Creek Hotel and its business cards.

Next morning I'm up early. It's our first day of School of the Air. I'm really excited, but I get the impression, after eight weeks of holidays, Ben would rather be somewhere else, riding his minibike out among the sand dunes or going on a bore run.

We sit at our desks and turn on the radio. The airwaves fill with music and voices, then the Principal comes on to say good morning to the entire school. The children all say good morning back. It's amazing to think that everyone we can hear right now is somewhere out there in the Northern Territory, so far away on cattle stations, in communities or with their families on roadwork gangs.

Ben presses the radio receiver in to say good morning too, and joins in on the Australian National Anthem. He's a little self-conscious, so I lean over and sing into the receiver with him. We don't sound too bad at all.

Assembly is over and Ben's radio lesson with his class is on air next.

'Good morning, students,' Mrs Simms' pleasant voice spills onto the airwaves.

'Good morning, Mrs Simms,' all the voices of Ben's class-mates respond at slightly different times.

Mrs Simms marks the role—everyone's present, except for someone who's out mending broken fences with their dad. Mrs Simms then asks everyone about their holidays. Ben tells her about Alice Springs. Then she talks about the year ahead, about school camp at Harts Range and sports day in Alice Springs. She encourages everyone to get their work done on time and send it in for marking in the green satchels each week.

'Talk with you all tomorrow. Bye, Year Four,' Mrs Simms closes.

'Bye, Mrs Simms!' all the voices chime.

Ben reaches over and turns the radio off and puts his chin in his hand. He's hot and tired, and so am I. We put off doing times tables and make it an early lunch instead. I race Ben over to the kitchen. The cook, 'Cookie', serves up cold meat, salad and bread and butter. He puts the platters out on the table and we wander along building delicious stacks of sandwiches.

Ben and I sit down to eat with Peter under the bough shed in the shade. I ask Peter about the drought.

'It's tough, but it's been tough like this before,' he says. 'The rain cycle is every seven to ten years, so it's a matter of hanging in there through the difficult, dry years until the clouds build and the rains appear and the cycle starts all over again.'

Hopefully the rains will come in the next few months.

The afternoon is hot—a blistering 42°C. We do math measurements with kitchen pots and pans in the shade of a gum tree and tip the water on ourselves when we're done. For afternoon smoko, everyone spends a whole lot of time in the kitchen coolroom 'looking for nothing in particular'.

Over the coming days Ben and I settle into our routine. I get the hang of the two-way radio, and Ben gets his first week's work packed up into the green school satchel and loaded into the mailbag. It will be delivered to Alice Springs for marking next week.

The weekend is here. Free time! Ben takes me exploring north of the homestead.

We watch as Peter checks the station's weather gauge for wind speed and direction, air and ground temperature and rainfall (there's none of that to record in his notebook). He walks back to the homestead to phone the results through to the Bureau of Meteorology.

We check on the twenty chooks in their dusty pen. Then climb through the old wooden stockyards and sit behind the steering wheels of old station vehicles. They're all rusted and broken from years of hard work. I think that's Peter's original truck from 1956 over there.

I phone home from the payphone next to the roadhouse. It's so good to hear Mum and Dad's voices. I fill them in on what I've been doing and they bring me up to speed with the world. I thank Mum for her ingenious Easter parcel of minties, instead of posting chocolate eggs that would have melted on the way. My coins clatter through quickly, and I wish I had more time to speak. I tell them I love them and tear up as the line cuts out.

Over the following weeks, Ben has a cooking class over the radio, a spelling and math test, and we tune in to listen to a guest speaker. We make a kite from an old bed sheet with a pair of pink polka dot stockings on the tail. But it blows away and we're left wondering if we'll ever see a steer strutting about in them — it would definitely help keep him safe crossing the road.

And as winter approaches I keep my promise with Ben, and we climb Mount Conner. It's an exhausting climb, but it's so worth it. We stand together on the tabletop and gaze out at the views, feeling immensely proud.

Out west, Uluru rises up magnificently from the flat desert floor. To the north, a chain of salt lakes paints white circles on the red sand. Over there we can see a tiny Curtin Springs homestead with its thin length of airstrip. I set up the tripod, press the timer on my camera and race into the picture with Ben. *Snap!* It captures a wonderful moment in time.

The winter weather brings cooler temperatures, but there is still no sign of rain. Curtin Springs remains in drought. The sunrises and sunsets stay in vivid hues due to the large amounts of dust in the air. Thankfully the water bores dotted around the property keep the water troughs filled for the cattle, but there's nothing that can be done about the diminishing feed on the ground.

There's talk of mustering. It goes on for a few weeks and then the date is set. Instead of hiring a helicopter and employing additional jackaroos on horseback or in 4WDs, it's done in a very clever way—water trapping. This method ends up being a lot less stressful for everyone, including the cattle.

So we pack our swags and food and drive out to the water bore on the eastern road to Mount Conner. It's late afternoon and the sun is sinking fast in our cloud of dust. Peter, Ben and I quietly check the yards and set up camp, and the cattle begin to mill around for their evening drink. Soon they wander in through a one-way trap, drinking at the troughs. But because the out trap is closed, they are caught in the yards. The plan from here will be: they'll be sorted, branded, released or loaded onto road trains.

Our swags are warm and waterproof. It's an amazing experience to sleep out under the stars with no roof to block out the view. Above us a new crescent moon shies away from the sky, and the ageing stars sparkle boldly. There's Orion's Belt, the Milky Way and of course the Southern Cross with the two pointers. Ben points out a shooting star and I watch a satellite trek across to the north.

We fall asleep to the sound of cattle mooing. Hopefully there'll be a good number in the yards in the morning.

In the east the morning sky is a magnificent red, fading up and away into a pale transparent blue. It's a sure sign that today, like all the other days this year, will be cloudless and warm. But it's not the sun that wakes me up, it's the flies!

I bury my head and hide in my swag, retreating like a frill-necked lizard behind a rock. But I have no choice, and I have to face them. We need to get up and check on the cattle then get back to the homestead. It's a weekday and that means school.

One by one we emerge from our swags. After breakfast we check the yards, and there's a good number of cattle. *Fantastic!*

As much as we'd like to stay, Ben and I head back to the station. He has a radio lesson at 9.30am and then tomorrow, Mrs Simms will be flying in. The pressure is on, we need to clean up the classroom and get some schoolwork done.

Our 4WD bounces along the dirt track back towards the Lasseter Highway, and the warm air blows onto our faces. I glance across at Ben. He gives me a smile back. We drive under a massive desert oak and Ben jumps out to open and close a gate. Soon we're barrelling back along the bitumen.

Curtin Springs homestead appears in the distance, nestled in among its garden of gum trees, its water tank and radio tower. It's my home for now and I love it here. I'm settling in, finding my place and learning the ropes.

Schoolwork with Ben is going well. I'm gaining confidence, becoming more resilient and I'm definitely not as shy as what I was, and I honestly know I don't talk like the queen!

On the odd days, when it feels like I'm stranded on a desert island, I write in my diary and I work on songs, and I walk along the airstrip with my walkman and its music, and that all helps me to get through.

I've come to realise that there's a whole incredible world out here in the outback, filled with opportunity and adventure, challenge and joy. We're not removed from everything, everything's just a long way from us ... and when I leave in December, to head home for Christmas, this fine, red dust, all these remarkable people, and all these memories that I share with them today, will remain with me forever.

*Chapter Four*

# THE TANAMI TRACK
# AND BEYOND

## *Two Journeys with Dad*

## JULY 1987

It's early, and both hands of my wristwatch are pointing downwards—it's half past seven. Here in Alice Springs the desert air is desperately cold. I can see my breath and it hangs in the air for a second or two. I'm already looking forward to my next cup of hot, milky tea, just like the one I had at breakfast. However, that may be a little while yet, as we have a long drive ahead.

To the east the winter sun is sitting squarely on the horizon. In fact, it's not moving much at all, it seems distracted, coaxing a handful of stubborn stars away from the fading canopy above.

Dad and I are loading up our last remaining bags. They're filled with clothing and food. The large containers of water go in last. We do a final check to make sure we've got everything, close the back of the 4WD, walk round one more time to check the tyres, and then climb in.

Dad and I are together again, heading off an adventure, just the two of us. It's the July school holidays, and I have four weeks off from my governess work at Curtin Springs. I'm really excited because this journey will give Dad the opportunity to pick up again from 1956, to explore an incredibly remote region of this country, which will link an undriven section for him and I'll be there right by his side.

I wriggle enthusiastically into the passenger side. But it's no warmer in here, and the chill from the grey vinyl seat creeps quickly into the empty back pockets of my jeans. I pull my jumper down for extra warmth, and stretch the woollen waistband as far as it'll go.

Dad eases in behind the steering wheel and turns the key in the ignition. The engine roars to life, it's like we're waking a snoring giant! He revs it gently to warm it up.

It's 7.55am. Time to go.

'Alright, Heather! Off we go, go, go, go, go, go!' That's Dad's little trademark singsong sentence, a family tradition, one he recites to mark the beginning of every road trip. He grins at me, his joy is palpable, and shifts into first gear. We're off.

Very soon our tyres are humming along the highway. It might not be the most comfortable ride, but this chunky 1978 Toyota 4WD of ours is as dependable and strong as the day is long, and here in the outback, that's exactly what we need.

On my lap sits a wrinkled old road map of Northern Australia. It's covered with meandering lines, joining the dots of unfamiliar towns and slicing through the squiggles of seasonal rivers. In between them, lies a whole lot of wide-open space.

But what I'm really looking at, is a long, intriguing line that heads diagonally up towards the dusty, dog-eared corner I'm clutching in my cold left hand. It's called the Tanami Track.

Dad's highlighted it in fluro orange, and for the next few days, that's where we'll be. We're heading off on an adventure, taking the longest shortcut in the entire country, all the way from the Red Centre to the Kimberleys in Western Australia, and leaving civilisation far, far behind.

In the ashtray, a handful of twenty cent coins rattle about. They're distracting. I scoop them out and put them in my pocket. Maybe they can buy us a cup of tea at the next roadhouse … hmmm … that is if there actually is one.

I settle back in my seat. Dad drives on. I'm feeling a whole lot warmer now. All around us, the red dirt and desert oaks stretch off to the horizon. This country peels open the sky like no other place in the world, giving the sun and the moon and the fleeting clouds far more room to play.

Up ahead a road train appears on a rise. We watch it grow bigger, more intimidating, with every passing second. Soon it's only metres away, racing towards us. Wisely, Dad moves over to the left. I hold my breath as it thunders past with its empty cattle trailers and multiple wheels. It's so heavy and fast that it creates its own cyclonic blast of buffeting air that shifts our 4WD further sideways and off the road.

Suddenly we're in the red dirt, bouncing and skidding on the rough, rutted shoulder. A long red plume of dust kicks up behind us, but Dad doesn't panic, he slows us down, keeps his hands firmly on the steering wheel and deftly guides us back onto the bitumen again.

Apart from the odd road train encounter, it's a straightforward journey right now. It's north from here up the Stuart Highway from Alice Springs, and in 20 kilometres or so, we'll take a left-hand turn onto Tanami Road. Then we'll trade in the bitumen for kilometres of dust and corrugations on the lonely stretch to Yuendumu.

Our journey beyond that? Well, who knows ... we're going it alone ... off into the wild frontier called the Tanami Desert. Am I worried? No, I'm not. I'm in great hands. My dad's a clever and capable man. He knows the workings of our 4WD, he's done his research on this route, and his track record stands at 100 per cent for getting us out of trouble before.

In the rear-vision mirror, the MacDonnell Ranges stand like an impenetrable, ochre army. But squint your eyes, and focus more closely, you'll see tiny chinks appear in their armour—tall narrow chasms carved out by ancient, persistent creeks, which are secret hiding places where rock wallabies climb and brown snakes bake, and through which weary stockmen and their horses wend their way home. But as mighty and as wide as these ranges are, they slip silently away to the south.

On our dashboard is a stash of simple displays: a speedometer, a temperature gauge, and two fuel gauges, one for the main tank and another for the reserve. Beneath them is a fast-turning odometer, and for the next four weeks it's got a job to do. It'll be busy ticking off every single kilometre that we travel.

I've also got a job to do, keeping up our travel log. It's a family tradition on these road trips. Dad buys an exercise book and writes up all our travel plans—the directions, campsites, fuel stops and sites of interest—all on the left-hand side. He leaves the right-hand side blank to record the distances actually driven, and to write any comments along the way. So while Dad drives, this is my homework, and I'll do it as diligently as I can in my increasingly smudgy, scrawly handwriting.

Out the window I catch my twenty-two-year-old reflection in the side mirror. I have no make up on, my hair's pulled back in a short, curly ponytail. Wrinkles haven't found me yet. I've got my mother's face and my father's eyes—it's always been that way. I haven't changed that much, just grown up I guess.

I glance over at Dad. He's concentrating on the road, not even aware that I'm looking at him. He's got his favourite checked flannelette shirt on, with the sleeves rolled back to his elbows. He doesn't feel the cold as much as I do. His 6.1-foot frame takes him so much closer to the cabin roof than any one of us who's ever travelled with him. On his jawline there's three-days growth of greying stubble, which, by the end of our four weeks together, will have grown into a half-decent beard. But, on his way home to Melbourne, to Mum, it will of course miraculously disappear!

Our engine roars on. We follow the mesmerising white lines flashing past on the wide, black highway. We drive all the way to the red horizon and beyond. On the edge of our bonnet sit two aerials that bend over backwards in the rushing air. The smaller one's for the local radio, for local news and weather updates, the larger one's our lifeline to the Royal Flying Doctor Service. We have an allocated call sign: 'Nine Victor Hotel … um, is it Tango … or Foxtrot … or Zulu?' I'm afraid I can't remember it and it probably isn't in that order either … just as well Dad has it all written down.

The road sign for the Tanami turn-off appears on the left. It reads Yuendumu 270 kilometres, Halls Creek 1032 kilometres. 'That's not too far,' I think out aloud, but I know I'm just kidding myself.

We turn off, bumping and jostling onto the track. Fine, red dust creeps in past the old rubber seals on the doors. It either settles on the dashboard or as grit in our teeth.

On the Tanami Track we encounter the odd sharp corner, with an exposed red bank and a fringe of spinifex, but mostly we're on long, straight sections filled with bull dust and parallel ruts. Dad negotiates them skillfully, switching from one side of the road to the other. Not once do we bottom out, not once do our tyres spin.

The hands on my wristwatch point upwards. It's now 9.05am. I fold the road map up and stow it in the glove box. It's pretty obvious where we're going right now—straight ahead. Dad drives on.

For the past six months, Dad and I have only had short conversations, straining to hear each other through the dusty, plastic handset of a long-distance pay phone at Curtin Springs. So finally, in what seems to be ages, Dad and I settle into a long, comfortable conversation.

We talk about Canada. I find out why we immigrated there in 1968—it looked like a great place to live, with lots of opportunities for a young family, amazing seasons and a beautiful landscape. Dad was particularly fascinated by the modern architecture and the fact that North America seemed so far ahead of its time. He wanted for us to be a part of it all.

We recollect the hanging baskets on the street lampposts overflowing with vibrant red flowers in summer. The golden maple leaves that grew crisp and then fell to the ground in autumn. Standing on the shores of the island as we watched rafts of logs float down from the forests, on their way to the wood mills. We'd chase them, balancing on the breakaways that had escaped earlier and washed up on the shore.

And of course we remember the snow of winter and how our driveway and garden disappeared beneath white. Real snow! We would help Dad shovel it off before busying ourselves building a snowman and playing on our sled. My mum's sense of fun shone through then too. She would lean out of the bathroom window and snap off icicles to eat as treats, wrapped up in white paper towels. And she was resourceful too. We didn't have waterproof boots so she made do by tying plastic bread bags over our shoes.

I find out why we returned in 1969—mostly because my Grandmother Elsie was dying from breast cancer. My mum must have been so relieved to be back by her side again.

We reminisce about our Easter caravan trips to Marysville, nestled in the Great Dividing Range. And the winding drive to get there, over The Black Spur, through tall, misty, enchanted eucalypt forests.

We laugh at the time we got the family station wagon bogged on an old disused logging trail on Lake Mountain, and the entire afternoon that we'd spent trying to get it out—laying long strips of bark and positioning flat rocks under the wheels for traction—but still our tyres spun, and the bark and rocks disappeared into the mire. So it was decided, all covered in mud and sweat, that we'd walk to the main road for help. And as a gentle snow fell, we hitchhiked our way back to town. The next day a tow truck retrieved our car from the mountain. Dad was relieved. Problem solved.

Dad and I also talk about our planned trips ahead. I am heading to Sydney to do a creative arts course to study drama and dance in 1988. I will support myself by nursing part-time. I know it's a completely new direction, which is a bit of a scary step, but I want to give it a go. From there, I'll see where life takes me … further north, maybe Canada, maybe even home.

Dad's keen to go to Antarctica and New Zealand with Mum.

Our conversation keeps coming back to two things—travel and home. Back to all those meandering lines and dots of our internal maps that keep us connected. To the dusty, dog-eared pages of our lives.

Our 4WD churns further north and the kilometres tick by. I sit in silence for a minute or two and wonder why we don't have more conversations like this in our daily lives.

The first of many signs to Rabbit Flat appears on the rise. It promises food, petrol and a safe place to stay. *Sounds great to me! I'm sure they'll have hot, milky tea.*

We turn off the track and ease through the open front gate and across the cattle grid to the property. The roadhouse is surrounded with gum trees, water tanks, petrol tanks and a long graded airstrip that doubles as a campsite—that's an interesting arrangement!

Rabbit Flat Roadhouse is built like a fortress and as soon as the sun sets and visitors have eaten their last mouthful of food or drunk their last beer, the doors and shutters are closed. If you're camping, you find yourself on the outside, on your own. It's a little disconcerting.

It's no surprise that Dad and I don't sleep very well, out on the airstrip alone. The desert air's filled with all sorts of sounds and a rattling road train thunders past around midnight. As the sky brightens in the east, we pack up our two-man tent. We don't want to be here when the mail plane lands!

'You can drive this morning,' Dad says.

'Okay,' I say, feeling the sudden weight of responsibility that comes with those words. I'm always a bit nervous to begin with when I hop into the driver's seat on rough roads like this, but a few kilometres in, I settle in.

We cross the border into Western Australia. We're making great headway. A snake slithers across the road. This is remote, wild country and the isolation seeps deep into your soul. Rusty road signs point off to distant mines.

The next stop on the track is Halls Creek, but that's still so many kilometres away. We keep an eye on the petrol gauge and Dad flicks the switch to our reserve petrol tank, timing it perfectly before our main tank empties. If all goes to plan, this will get us now all the way through.

The long, red, dusty track stretches on. Wolfe Creek meteorite crater rises up on the right. We stop and take some photos. Dad climbs up the ladder onto the roof racks to get a better shot. It's a massive dent in the earth. A perfect circle made by outer space.

The sun treks west and into our eyes. It's time to find a place to camp, so we pull off the road about 25 kilometres on. We set up our tent and have tinned spaghetti and rehydrated peas, carrots and mashed potato, and a cup of tea.

The next day is our last day on the dust and corrugations. We share the driver's seat and watch the fuel gauge. It's a very long day, but finally we reach the smooth, welcoming bitumen of the main road north and turn right to Kununurra. *We've made it!*

A few days later, fuelled with fresh supplies and petrol, we head in to the Bungle Bungles National Park. It's a rough track, and we bounce and rattle along. *How far until we'll see the beehive-like domes?* Expectations are running high.

We're not disappointed. There they are, standing like an ancient, stripy, city with its seasonal waterway called Piccaninny Creek. According to Dad's research, and from this morning's conversation with the new park ranger, if you follow this riverbed deep into the domes, you'll find a gorge with towering walls and tranquil waterholes.

'Are you up for this, Heather?' Dad asks.

'Yes, I am,' I reply.

So we pack. We fill our backpacks with food, with sleeping bags, and all the drink containers we can possibly carry. It's a warm July morning and the sun is bright. I'm glad we have our hats on. We walk along rutted, weathered sandstone sprinkled and filled with smooth pebbles and flood debris.

Soon we disappear into the cooler shadows of the mounds. I trace my hand along the horizontal layers and wander deeper, further in. The ochre sandstone glows back at us in the reflective light. Apart from a rock wallaby watching from up high, there's no one else here ... it's silent, powerfully silent.

As the day wears on, the creek bed takes us over boulders, around bends, and eventually into the presence and the magnificence of Piccaninny Gorge. The walls are sheer and high. *It's breathtaking.* Pencil-thin palm trees stretch from one side of the gorge to the other, and at its base, still, reflective pools copy and paste the vibrant colour of the sky.

'This is what I wanted to see,' says Dad. 'This is really, really special and it's definitely worth every single dusty kilometre that we drove along the Tanami Track.' He pauses to take photos, then repositions to take more.

I sit and eat apples on a rock and soak it all in. As the sky reddens and the day slips away, we set up our camp in the gorge. Above us the eager stars crowd together to fill the tiny slice of sky. For a short while I can see the Southern Cross, the pointers and the Milky Way. But more stars appear over the eastern edge and push them out of view. One by one they trek along their own path to the western wall, to disappear too.

We lay in our sleeping bags on the river pebbles and talk and stare skywards ... and eventually drift off to sleep. I didn't know it at the time, and it wasn't until several years later, that this was to be one of the most treasured journeys I'd ever have with my dad.

In 2011, twenty-three years after this Tanami trip, we lost Dad to mesothelioma. He fought valiantly, trying his very best to keep his track record of 100 per cent for getting out of trouble. He had surgery, and he had chemotherapy. It gave him two and a half more years.

With my brothers, Trevor and Ray, and our families, we nursed him through the final weeks of his life, staying true to our promise to keep him at home.

We gave him pain relief, managed his oxygen, gently fed and bathed him. We reminisced when we could and told him we loved him through our growing, spilling tears.

We took turns to sit in the armchair next to his bed. Sitting in the 'passenger seat' one more time, together for this one last undriven journey. We looked across at him and remembered the strong, clever, capable man that he was, that he still was inside, and that he always would be.

But sadly our long conversations became shorter—he was out of breath. He was tiring quickly. These were difficult days framed by long, sleepless nights.

Soon Dad slipped quietly into unconsciousness, and a couple of days later, after the winter sun had set on a cool July evening, he was gone.

In the following days, we organised his funeral and began to slowly pack up his world. It was an internal tug of war being practical and emotional at the same time. There were so many decisions to make and so many memories to relive. I was so glad I didn't have to face it alone.

As I sat at Dad's computer, writing my part of his eulogy, it struck me that being here for him in his final few months of life was one of the biggest achievements in my life so far. It still is. It always will be.

In that final letter to Dad, I told him I loved him. I wrote about Canada and Marysville and our trip along the Tanami Track to the Bungle Bungles. About our long conversations and the stars … all those stars that had drifted past Piccaninny Gorge on their way up to heaven.

And something tells me that there's more than just stars in heaven—there's red dirt and vast horizons, and it's crisscrossed with adventurous tracks and little dots of towns, and riverbeds that overflow to make rain. Dad will be loading up the 4WD, getting out the crinkled road map and picking up exactly where he left off with Mum. He'll be driving and she'll be navigating in the passenger seat.

They'll be having long conversations and stopping to watch the winter sun as it sits squarely on the westerly horizon, not moving much at all, distracted. They'll be the ones coaxing a handful of stubborn stars back into the majestic, deepening blue canopy of the sky, to encourage us to keep looking up, to keep dreaming of adventure, and to remind us of all those journeys we've travelled together.

*Chapter Five*

# SETTLING IN

*A New Stage in Life*

## JANUARY 1988 – DECEMBER 2006

My knuckles are white. I haven't adjusted my steely grip on the steering wheel of my mint green hatchback for at least half an hour. For the very first time in my life, I'm finding myself planted squarely in the middle of peak-hour traffic on Pittwater Road. I'm lost in a chaotic world of brake lights and traffic lights in Australia's largest city—Sydney. Right now I'm so far out of my comfort zone, it's not funny, and so far away from all those easygoing red, dusty tracks of the outback. I'm stressed to the point I even have to remind myself to blink.

Up ahead I seek out the solace of a side street and pull over to catch my breath and check my road map. I trace the long winding line on the page with my shaking finger and figure out that I'm not actually lost, but there's still a few more kilometres to go until Avalon. From there it'll be a left-hand turn to get to Clareville, and then it's hopefully not too far to the house where I'll be living for the next eight months. I'll be staying with a wonderful older nurse called Margaret.

I finally locate her street and see a little white letterbox in a garden bed with the silver number three. I pull in and peel my fingers away from this wheel. Margaret greets me with a smile in the driveway and immediately puts me at ease. There's just something so very familiar about her, she reminds me so much of my mum.

It's late January 1988, and I'm here in Sydney trying out something new. Actually, make that two things. I want to see what it's like to live in a big, unfamiliar city—a complete contrast to the outback—and I'm keen to cultivate my creativity by studying drama and dance. It's time to stretch myself and step beyond those smaller street theatre and musical productions that I performed in as a teenager.

But in the background I'll remain practical. I'll keep up my nursing skills and support myself by working part-time as a community nurse.

Over the next few weeks I settle into the course. I make new friends and get a whole lot better at driving in the Sydney traffic, even surviving a drive over the Sydney Harbour bridge to the Opera House! I study acting techniques and learn about the specific roles, on stage and on set, of theatre and film productions. I study Shakespeare, as well as more contemporary plays. I learn how to do jazz ballet (reasonably well), and tap dance (perhaps not so well). In the evenings and on weekends I nurse a number of disabled and terminally ill patients in their own homes. Their families become my close friends too.

But as the months fly by, I start to think about travelling again. About getting back out onto country roads and finding freedom. I'm happy that I've explored this creative sidestep, and enjoyed the experience of living in Sydney, but I'm ready to move on. I firm up my plans to head north to Queensland. But then Doug unexpectedly walks into my world …

It's Wednesday morning and we've been told to expect a visitor, called Doug Hawkins, in our drama class. He's here to workshop a script with us, one that he's been writing for a short film, called *The Third Wave*. He's also the producer on the production. Just after 9am the door opens and in he walks wearing a very cool leather jacket and stonewash jeans. I can't help but stare. It's definitely love at first sight. I blush big time and all I can think about is: *great, of all days, I've chosen to wear a pair of big baggy shorts, hiking boots and my curls are frizzing out of control in the humidity.*

Throughout the session we exchange banter and lingering looks but for some odd reason, maybe due to the pull and distraction of all the other people on the day, we don't exchange phone numbers. I drive home feeling cross at myself. I know I've missed a big opportunity.

To my surprise, Doug comes to our course graduation ceremony the following week. He has in his hand six red roses, and in his heart the intent of asking me out. But what he sees, makes his spirits sink; I'm already holding a *dozen* red roses. He thinks they're from another guy. But actually they're from Margaret!

Then there's another false start, when Doug rings my number and mistakenly thinks I'm married with children. However, we finally get it together and go out on our first date—dinner and movies at The Cremorne Orpheum.

So our unexpected relationship blossoms, and this alters my travel plans enormously. I'm suddenly feeling a change, a rearrangement in my heart. I can't leave Sydney now, as I have to stay to see how things play out. So I do. I keep nursing and also successfully audition for a role in a play at the Genesian Theatre Company. But it's no surprise that I give up tap dancing!

Throughout this time Doug lives and breathes the pre-production of his film, he has an incredible amount of work to do. There are days we don't see or speak with each other, but despite this, our relationship continues to thrive.

Filming for *The Third Wave* is soon scheduled for March 1989. I'm contracted to work as the unit nurse on crew and appear in a couple of background scenes as an extra. In the final edit it's easy to pick me out from the crowd with my crazy hair.

Things move pretty fast from here. In November 1989, Doug meets my parents for the very first time and in less than four hours has asked them permission for my hand in marriage. They give their blessing. We get engaged, and then on the 31 March 1990, we marry. It's whirlwind, but we're in love and we're ready to make the commitment.

We rent a semi-detached house in Coogee, three blocks from the beach. After all those years of living near the mountains in Montrose, and travelling in the outback, it's a fabulous contrast to be settling next to the boundless, blue Pacific Ocean.

Two years later, in 1992, we do three things all at once—we buy a car, buy a two-bedroom unit a few blocks away, and we have our first beautiful baby, Rebekah (Bek). Thankfully things have changed since 1965, and Doug, and my mum, are allowed into the labour ward with me. It means so much to share such an intense, profound experience with them, and they help me cope with the pain of birth. It also means there'll be no need for my obstetrician Dr Christopher Bradbury to knock on our front window to tell Doug the news!

Two and a half years later, in April 1995, we do the same three things again, nearly—we buy another car, move a few blocks away, but this time I give birth to a boy, Callum (Cal).

It's in here, in the labour ward of the Royal Women's Hospital, in the most unexpected place in the world, that I catch a glimpse of my love of rising up to a challenge.

It's late evening, Easter Saturday, and my labour is progressing steadily. The midwife pops in frequently to check on me. All is going well. Then one time when she's taking my blood pressure, she happens to mention that the first baby born after midnight will be named the Easter Baby and be presented with a hamper of giant chocolate Easter eggs. Now if that's not enough encouragement to get things happening, then I don't know what is! But I'm not alone in this quest, there just so happens to be a lady in the adjacent room up to a similar stage in her labour.

As the night progresses, the midwife moves between rooms giving us encouragement like a footy coach. This adds a whole new dimension to my birth experience. (They didn't talk about this in our pre-natal classes.) I ease off the pain relief gas and focus up and push steadily, when I'm told to, that is. The thought of chocolate eggs fills my head … Keep going. Breathe. Push. Breathe. Push. Push!

At 2.15am we welcome Cal into our arms, along with a glorious basket of Easter eggs, a visit from the Channel 7 news team and the Easter bunny!

We're ecstatic! Our family is complete.

With a toddler and a baby in the house, our days are filled with love and joy, but also never-ending nappy changes, sleepless nights, a lounge room filled with toys, and long disorganised days still found in our pyjamas. But we get through. Both our parents provide strong emotional support and practical tips, and are the best babysitters ever. I recognise that the way that I parent, is based so much upon the way my mum and dad brought me up.

Every now and then my thoughts drift off to travelling, and I imagine what the rest of Australia might have been like had I kept to my original plans. But my heart keeps drawing me back in to the new adventure that I'm living in right now. To the one I would not swap for this entire world—the experience of being a wife, a mother, and a quarter of this precious, unique, indivisible family equation.

The years go by. For nineteen of them, Doug and I work together in our film and video production company and watch our children grow up. These are busy years, but great years. Doug heads up the business as Producer and Director, and I manage the office and financial accounts between the hours of 9am – 3pm. We've structured it this way so I can pick Bek and Cal up from school. We produce documentaries, training films, television advertisements, and we create numerous videos for the National Museum of Australia—we're incredibly proud of this historically significant body of work and it's a career highlight to be on the list of invited guests at the official opening of the museum in 2001.

We have frequent trips to Montrose to see my mum and dad, to the house where I grew up. Bek and Cal play in the paddocks and race up and down the gravel driveway where my brothers and I barrelled down on our billycarts. They share bedtime stories with Grandma and Grandpa, and catch up with their cousins. They sit and listen to the pine trees sigh, and look out across the valley to the mountains. They study the souvenirs on the built-in wall unit, and read the names on all the boxes of slides—all those things that I'd done as a child. And soon they too begin to dream of travel and adventure ...

But as with sunlight, there can also be shade, and sometimes life can bring unexpected change. Little do we know, the incredibly profound, life-changing challenge that our family is about to face.

*Chapter Six*

# OVARIAN CANCER

*My World is Changed Forever*

## DECEMBER 2006 – MARCH 2007

'I really don't like this middle-age spread business.' I turn to Bek and point with both hands towards my tummy. My black one-piece swimsuit seems tighter around the middle than it was a couple of weeks ago. I must be putting on weight.

It was bound to happen, I guess, nearly forty-two, not exercising much, and I imagine it's a sign of things to come – middle-age spread, then menopause …

'Oh Madre,' Bek replies (it's Spanish for Mum and it's what she's called me ever since her school exchange to Madrid) giving me a reassuring hug. 'You've got ages to go until you get there!'

I hug her back and say, 'I wish!'

We laugh out loud and gaze out to sea, while a wave sneaks away with our footprints.

'How about a couple more laps,' I suggest to Bek, hoping it'll make a difference to my waistline. So we walk down to the south end, all the way to the spilling ocean pool, and then back through the shallows to the headland.

It's a perfect Friday afternoon at Coogee, and the time on the surf club wall says 5.30pm. People are flocking to the sand with their colourful towels, clocking off from work to add a restorative swim to the end of their week. While over on the steps, in among the squadrons of seagulls, families are clutching tightly to their paper parcels of hot fish and chips. Bek and I take off our sunglasses and ease into the waves. *Ah … this is so lovely and refreshing.* I'm so happy that the weekend is here. Christmas is upon us—only two weeks to go.

At work on Monday, my favourite red skirt feels uncomfortable. My waistband seems a little tight. I wriggle it up higher. *Did I really eat that much over the weekend, or did it shrink in the dryer?*

The afternoon drags on. I'm off to bathroom more times than not and the humidity makes me exceptionally tired. That night my period starts and it's a whole lot heavier than normal. *Perhaps that explains what's going on with my waist!*

Only one week until Christmas.

My mum and dad fly in from Melbourne and they stay with us for a week and a half. We celebrate Christmas and the new year together. We decorate the house, go shopping for presents, have picnics and walks in the Botanical Gardens. We watch the fireworks and welcome in 2007.

'Here's to a good year!' we say to each other and tumble into bed before midnight.

I make a new year's resolution to watch my weight, not eat as much chocolate and to exercise more. The days together fly by. As we say goodbye to my parents at the airport gate, I'm incredibly emotional, a little more than normal. Tears keep flowing for an unusually long time.

Three weeks after Christmas, I have another heavy period. This time there's even more severe abdominal cramping and bloating. It's horrible. I'm up a lot at night to go to the bathroom. *Maybe I've missed middle-age spread and headed straight into menopause?*

Summer holidays drift away and the school year begins. Bek starts in year nine and Cal in year six. Life powers back up into a hectic routine of early mornings, afternoon sports and homework. And at work, Doug and I settle into another busy year. He has scripts to write and videos to produce, and I've got the finances and the office to manage.

On Wednesday morning, I can't fit into my red skirt *at all*, and this really upsets me. It's not a great start to the day, and I tear up as I hang it back up in the wardrobe. I question myself. *Why have I put on so much weight? Has my metabolism changed that much? I don't understand …* But what I do understand is that I've got to stick to my new year's resolution diet, and give up chocolate, completely—now that makes me sad.

Friday afternoon, Bek and I go for a longer walk and swim at the beach.

Sunday morning, we have a much-needed sleep in. I'm first up to have a shower around 9.00am. As I undress in the bathroom, I see my silhouette in the mirror. It's alarming—I actually look pregnant.

*What? What on earth is going on? I've been having periods … we have our contraception worked out …*

I need to dust off my nursing skills and seek out some clues. So instead of showering, I lay back on the bed to examine my tummy. I follow the technique I learnt all those years ago, of dividing the abdomen into four equal quadrants.

I start by prodding above my belly button to the left and then the right—it all feels normal and soft. I press in on my lower-left side, and that's normal too. I press in on my lower-right side—it's firm. It feels different. It's uncomfortable to touch. A wash of anxiety spreads through my body.

'Doug! Doug! Wake up!' I shake his shoulder. 'There's something I need to tell you! There's something wrong!'

The rest of our Sunday is a blur. We try to act as normal as possible. We swim at the beach and do the food shopping for the week. We cook a roast dinner and watch a movie. But when the kids are in bed and the lights are turned out that night, Doug and I really struggle to sleep.

Monday morning I put on my favourite loose floral blouse and chocolate-brown skirt. We drive to our office in Surry Hills. Doug starts on some production work, while I drop Bek and Cal at school. I'm back through the traffic in no time to make a 9am phone call to our family doctor—Dr John Kearney.

I sit at my desk, and take in a deep breath and dial. Dr Kearney's wife, Helene, who's also the medical receptionist, answers the phone. She's known me for seventeen years.

'Hi Helene, can I make an appointment as soon as possible?' I ask in a shaky voice.

'Yes, Heather,' she says, picking up on my anxiousness. 'Come in at 11am.'

I have an hour to concentrate on work, but all I do is move things around my desk and drink cups of tea.

I keep feeling the firmness in my abdomen. *It must be an ovarian cyst,* I tell myself, *because with appendicitis there'd be a whole lot more pain. Either way, it will probably mean surgery, which I just don't have time for right now …*

Doug and I let our staff know we'll be an hour or so. They wish me all the best, and then we drive to North Bondi.

Dr Kearney divides my abdomen into four equal quadrants and prods and taps and looks concerned. 'Yes, there's definitely a firmness there in that lower-right quadrant.'

We sit down together and come up with a plan.

'You need to have a CT scan, a chest x-ray and some bloods taken,' Dr Kearney outlines.

'Okay,' I respond, taking it all in.

'So, let's get you in for these scans first.' Dr Kearney picks up the phone and calls the local radiology centre on my behalf. He explains the situation. They'll see me straight away. *Perfect!*

We'll have the results by this afternoon, so for now I'm relieved. The sooner we know, the sooner we can deal with whatever it is.

Doug and I arrive at Bondi radiology and check-in. I have to drink a litre of water before my CT scan. So I sit in the chair next to the water dispenser and keep topping up my little plastic cup. Doug's by my side. We flip through pictures in a travel magazine while we wait. *Wouldn't Canada be lovely right now …*

I hear my name and change into a white backless hospital gown. All of a sudden I'm transformed into a patient and I really don't like this. I have my chest x-rayed first. That's all very straightforward. Then it's time for my CT scan in the room next door.

The radiologist is chatty and she talks me through the process. 'We'll inject you with a contrast dye. You may experience a slight metallic taste in your mouth and will possibly feel flushed and light-headed.'

'Okay,' I respond. I lay on the bed with my arms by my side. The roundness of my abdomen is so evident under my gown. I look at it and wonder how I got here—from feeling so healthy a few weeks ago, to looking like this. I struggle to hold back my tears. The bed shifts me into the barrel of the scanner. It's like I'm on the inside of a giant digital camera. It whirrs and moves and clicks.

I listen to the radiologist's instructions: 'Hold your breath … okay, breathe now. You're going really well, Heather. I'll tell you to do this again in a moment.'

We repeat this process several times. I close my eyes and imagine all the images this machine is capturing, all the slices of my life, all so neatly stacked in a row.

'Hold your breath … okay, now breathe.'

As the minutes tick by, the radiologist's voice becomes noticeably subdued and I have a sense that something is wrong.

'Heather, breathe in, hold your breath … now breathe. That's it, dear. Stay there for a moment, we'll just check all the scans and then you'll be free to go,' she advises me over the intercom.

I lay still, staring at the machinery, trying not to jump to any conclusions.

A minute or so later, I hear her say, 'Okay, we're all finished.'

The bed slides out from the barrel and stops. I stand up, and the door to the room opens up.

'Thank you, Heather, take care,' the radiologist says, putting a hand on my shoulder as I leave. *What exactly has she seen?*

We settle the account at the front desk and arrange to come back in an hour to pick up the films and the full report. By then the results will have been faxed to Dr Kearney.

Doug and I wander to a nearby café and order a coffee and a raspberry friand. I sit and stir my latte and eat the froth from the top. We're both quiet and numb.

'Well, whatever it is, we'll face this together,' Doug says, looking me straight in the eye. 'Remember, Heather, I'm here for you. Bek and Cal are here for you. As are you're mum and dad and brothers. You're not alone.'

Tears well up in my eyes and I put my head in my hands. Doug gets up and envelops me in his arms. We finish our coffee. An hour finally passes.

The large white envelope, with my scans inside, sits at the front desk at radiology. It's sealed, and I choose to leave it that way. I pick it up and we drive to Dr Kearney's rooms.

It's afterhours but they've kept the surgery open just for us. Helene looks up from her reception desk. She's very pale. 'The fax has come through. Please go straight in to see John.'

I catch my breath.

Dr Kearney is at his desk, reading the report. He turns and greets us quietly. His eyes are moist. We take a seat and Doug grasps my hand.

Dr Kearney takes off his glasses and speaks gently. 'Heather, dear, I'm so sorry to tell you this news—it appears you have a large, complex tumour on your right ovary.'

His words hang up in the air. I honestly don't know what to say. I look over at Doug and his eyes are welling up. I look back at Dr Kearney, his are too.

I'm in shock. We're all in shock.

There's silence.

Then all my questions come tumbling out.

'What's my prognosis? Is it benign? Is it cancerous? Has it spread? I guess this will mean surgery? Will I need chemotherapy? Will I even survive this?'

But we really don't have answers for these questions yet. However, one thing I do know is that it's a far more serious situation than I ever imagined.

*Maybe my life is over … finished … gone at forty-two. It's not that I'm frightened of dying; it's just that I'm not ready to go. There's still so much I want to do, and like every other parent on this planet, I want to be here to see my children grow up.*

In the past, I've coped with tough times by getting practical. *I've got to get practical again.* I need an outlet for all my emotions and it will keep the growing fear inside of me under control. *I don't want to feel helpless. I want something to do.*

'Heather, I'll refer you to see a gynaecological surgeon. I know just the person,' Dr Kearney advises. 'It's Dr Christopher Bradbury, he operates at St Vincent's Hospital.'

'Dr Christopher Bradbury!' I respond. 'He was my obstetrician. He delivered Bek fourteen years ago. I'll be in great hands!'

Dr Kearney picks up the phone and calls Dr Bradbury's rooms on my behalf.

*Good. That's organised. He'll see me on Thursday morning. That's so soon.* I am relieved we can get things happening so quickly.

All I need now is to get my bloods taken tomorrow morning so the results will be ready for Thursday. One thing they'll be looking for is the ovarian cancer tumour marker—CA125. This is the first time I hear these two letters and three numbers, and from here on they become the yardstick of my life.

We hug Dr Kearney and Helene. They insist the appointments today are free of charge. I can't thank them enough for their care.

Doug and I walk out into the late afternoon. The peak-hour traffic is building and the sun is heading west. Everything seems perfect, so ordered, unchanged—there are busy lanes of buses and cars and brakelights. Yet for us, our world feels far from perfect, out of kilter, completely changed. We've been thrust into the centre ring, preparing for the fight of our lives.

We wait until we're at home to tell Bek and Cal, and all sit together on the lounge. We're honest with them and tell them that it's an ovarian tumour and that I'll need to have surgery as soon as possible. They're both very quiet and pale, trying their best to figure out what this now means for our world. I manage to keep it together by speaking in practical terms and using positive words, but the moment they take me in their arms, I crumble apart and we all have a very long cry.

'How can I tell Mum and Dad?' I ask, sitting sobbing and staring at the phone. I can't even compose myself, let alone compose a few words. How do you tell your parents that you've probably got cancer?

'Let me help you,' Doug gently picks up the handset and dials their number.

Dad answers and together Doug and I break the news. There are many tears, but at least we can tell them there's a plan in place and we have a handful of hope. Next, we call my brothers and talk things through.

These are the hardest calls we've ever had to make. That's all we do for now. We'll let other people in our world know over the coming days. Tonight we need to cope with it ourselves, and simply bunker down and be a family.

The next morning I have my bloods taken. The nurse asks me what my name is, my date of birth and looks at the pathology request. She reads it out aloud, deciphering Dr Kearney's handwriting, 'hCG, Alpha-fetoprotein, LDH and CA125', and looks across at me empathetically.

It's quite a shopping list, and those last two letters and three numbers give it away as to why I'm here. She prepares the vials and the syringe. I look the other way as she inserts the needle into my arm, as I honestly can't bear to watch.

We head into our office in Surry Hills along our usual route. I drop Doug off to catch up on yesterday's calls and emails, and then I drive Bek and Cal to school. I turn the radio down, there's way too much going on in my head.

As the days pass, my abdomen continues to swell. By the time Thursday comes around, I look like I'm five months pregnant. I'm quickly running out of clothes to wear. There are two free-flowing summer dresses that I still fit into, but anything with a waistband is out. In the corner of my wardrobe, my red skirt sits unused on its hanger. 'One day,' I promise myself, 'I'll wear that again.'

With my CT scan, chest x-ray and my referral on my lap, Doug and I wait in Dr Bradbury's consulting rooms. I remember this place well, with its comfortable chairs and its views over the Paddington rooftops. Last time I was here I was pregnant with Bek. That was 1992. I could never have imagined I'd be back fifteen years later, looking pregnant again, but for a whole different reason.

Dr Bradbury welcomes us warmly. 'I do remember you, Heather,' he says. 'But as lovely as it is to see you, I'm sorry for it to be under these circumstances.'

I pass him the scans and he studies them closely. He checks my blood results online. The CA125 levels are elevated. My heart sinks ... my tumour is cancerous. It completely dashes any hope left inside that the tumour would be benign. I glance across at Doug and reach out for his hand. I need to feel his warmth, and draw from his strength, because my lifeblood feels like it's draining away.

He examines my abdomen in the four different quadrants. He confirms the firmness on the right-hand side. 'Well, Heather, you do need surgery as soon as possible. I'm recommending you have a total abdominal hysterectomy and a bilateral salpingo-oophorectomy, along with removal of part of your omentum.'

These are long medical words, but thanks to my nursing training I understand what they're all about. I'll have surgery to remove my uterus, my ovaries and my fallopian tubes, along with a portion of my omentum—the fatty tissue that covers and supports the intestines and organs in my lower abdomen.

It's not a hard decision. It's going to save my life. Besides, Doug and I have two amazing children, we're not planning to have anymore. I guess with any surgery there is a risk that things can go wrong. But it's a chance I'll have to take. It will mean I'll head straight into menopause, but that can be handled with hormones. It will mean I have no more periods, now that's a positive, so that seals the deal!

Surgery is scheduled for next Wednesday, 7 March—six days time. Doug squeezes my hand. I squeeze it back.

In the interim I need to have an ultrasound to get some more detailed measurements of the tumour, and general bloods in preparation for surgery.

A practical plan is in place. I can't wait to get this stage over and done with. I can't wait to get this tumour removed, and I'm desperately hoping it doesn't spread any further before then. I pull myself up from thinking too much about the cancer inside and becoming paralysed with fear. It's now a matter of keeping it together for the next six days, staying as calm and as positive as I can. Getting as much work done at the office, praying and focusing on doing normal family things. Then from next Wednesday, we'll face the future from there. I'm ready and I'm beginning to sense there is a way through.

We tell our neighbours and close friends and we fly along on autopilot for the next few days.

I have the ultrasound on Monday. The tumour has grown. It's pushing my uterus across to the left side of my abdomen.

Two days to go.

I get as much work done as possible and tidy my office desk for one last time and shut my computer down.

One day to go.

Tuesday night I call Mum and Dad and my brothers. We say a family prayer before we say goodnight to the kids. I pack my hospital bag.

*Tomorrow will be here soon. It will bring change.*

I can't eat or drink anything from midnight onwards. In fact, I don't sleep much at all, as my swollen abdomen is really uncomfortable. I position a few pillows for support, but even then I can't drift off. My mind is whirring. *Will Bek and Cal be okay today? How will things run smoothly with accounts at the office? Will I be alive this time next year?* I watch the clock on my bedside table count my life away. Somewhere around 2.30am I finally fall asleep.

I wake up at dawn really hungry and lay there and listen to the morning birds. It's a beautiful, crisp autumn day. I hold TG the Bear close. It would be so lovely to go for a coastal walk and spend the morning by the sea—to breathe in the ocean air and have conversations about hopes and dreams and the future, and normal things like what to cook for dinner. I'm not ready to leave all of this behind.

But it's time to go.

Soon we're in among the morning traffic along Oxford Street. All around us people are going about their daily lives. It's surreal to think that mine's on hold right now and we're not going in to work today.

*The original 'Adventurous Spirit', my dad 1956.*

*Passport to a new life in Canada.*

*The Grand Canyon 1969.*
CREDIT: BOB INGAMELLS

*First day of primary school 1970.*
CREDIT: BOB INGAMELLS

*Ben Severin and myself at the cairn on top of Mt Conner, Curtin Springs Cattle Station 1987.*
CREDIT: HEATHER HAWKINS

*Just married!*
CREDIT: THE PICTUREMAN

*Easter Sunday 1995 with Bek, my mum, newborn Cal and all those Easter eggs!*
CREDIT: DOUG HAWKINS

*With Bek and Cal in 1997.*
CREDIT: DOUG HAWKINS

*Early days recovering from surgery.*
CREDIT: REBEKAH HAWKINS

*Mother's Day Classic fun run 2013 with Bek and Cal.*

*First marathon, Sydney, September 2013.*

*Training for the North Pole Marathon on Coogee Beach.*

CREDIT: HEATHER HAWKINS

*With Doug in our patrol gear at Longyerbyen, Norway. A freezing cold -26°C.*

CREDIT: ED CARTY

We arrive at St Vincent's Hospital and Doug, Bek and Cal come up with me to the waiting area on the ward. The nurse takes my blood pressure, pulse, and temperature—all seems good. I'm given a patient wristband. The anaesthetist checks my chest and my breathing—again all seems good.

I'm given a hospital gown. A final trip to the bathroom, and then I have my pre-med medication. Very soon I start to feel sleepy.

Everyone gives me a final hug. I kiss them goodbye and tell them I love them. Someone's tears drip down onto my hospital gown. I try to steady my breathing and tell myself that it's time to be brave. Brave for Doug, Bek and Cal, for my brothers and my mum and dad.

As the hospital orderly and nurse wheel me away along the corridor to the lifts, I smile and wave and reassure my precious family that I'll see them all again soon.

There's a few minutes to wait outside the operating suites, so I lay on my hospital trolley with my arms by my side. The roundness of my abdomen is even more evident under my gown. So many emotions are surging through my body right now. My heart is racing. Fear is trying to creep back in. I'm trying to be strong. There is a vigorous tug of war between immense relief that the day is finally here, but apprehension about how the surgery will go and more importantly, what it will reveal. Everything revolves around that. My world. My life. My future. Will my days from here be counted in weeks instead of years?

Dr Bradbury appears beside me. He takes a hold of my hand to tell me something important. 'Heather,' he says earnestly, 'you've walked into a storm, but I'll be with you and I'll bring you all the way through.' His words wrap around me like prayer flags. I know I'm in safe hands.

I have my family, my surgeon, faith and the power of everyone's love and prayers. As he walks away through the doors, to scrub up for surgery, my eyes fill with tears. They run down my cheeks and wash away any remaining fragments of fear. I don't wipe them away, but drift off to sleep, safe in the knowledge that he'll find a way through.

It's a big operation. Dr Bradbury makes a large abdominal incision from my belly button down. The tumour is situated within a cyst on my right ovary. It's 18 centimetres in diameter and weighs an alarming 1.25 kilograms and confirms what the scans have said—it's a fast-growing immature teratoma with several scattered areas of cancer within its tissues.

He skillfully removes the mass without rupturing the cyst walls, then performs a total hysterectomy and takes out my other ovary and fallopian tube. He methodically separates a large section of the fatty omentum from the front of my abdominal cavity. A sample of peritoneal fluid is taken and the wound is closed.

Dr Christopher has taken away so much, but in return, he's given me back so much—my life!

Everything is sent off to pathology for investigation and it will determine where my world goes to from here.

I hear the nurse's voice calling my name and I open my eyes. I look around and realise I'm in the recovery ward. *The operation is over; the tumour is gone. I'm alive—I'm so relieved about that!*

But I'm also in a lot of pain. The rawness radiating from my abdomen makes me sob uncontrollably. I try my best to keep it together, but the pain is overwhelming. The nurse gives me additional pain relief via my intravenous drip, and I drift off to sleep again for a little while ...

I hear the nurse's voice again.

'What time is it?' I ask. 'Is it still the same day?'

Shortly afterwards I'm wheeled to the ward and to my room. They align the hospital trolley up next to my bed, and even though the staff offer me a helping hand, the journey across seems more like a marathon.

The nurse pulls up the cot sides and I curl up into a vulnerable little ball beneath the starched cotton sheets. I'm desperate for the solace of sleep.

I'm unaware a few minutes later that Doug and Bek come into my room. They can't see me beneath the covers. The nurse reassures them I'm there and gently peels back my sheet and wakes me up.

It's so lovely to see their faces and to feel their kisses on my forehead. They've brought a beautiful bunch of yellow roses. They sit and hold my hand. A diet of soup, raspberry jelly and a cup of tea arrives on my tray table. I manage to drink the tea. I put the jelly to the side—I'll have that in a little while.

Doug phones my parents and lets them know I'm out of surgery and back in the ward. He puts them on speaker. The relief in their voices makes me cry. If only I could hold them right now.

Doug picks Cal up from school. I share my jelly with him and then start to get sleepy. It's 6pm. Doug, Bek and Cal head home for dinner. They're all exhausted too—it's been a very big day, a tough day, a life-changing day for us all.

I sleep fitfully. Every time I move it stirs up the pain, but I know I need to shift, to ease the pressure and the stiffness in my limbs. It's a tricky balance. I self-administer my morphine drip as best I can and in between I try to sleep.

I listen to the sounds of the ward and watch as the pale morning light filters in through the window. It's Thursday, 8 March 2007. It's a brand-new day.

The activity on the ward increases. A new nurse introduces herself. I'm in new hands. She helps me wash and take off my sweaty hospital gown. I change into my clean colourful nightie and I feel a whole lot better. I comb my hair and brush my teeth. *Now that looks more like the Heather I normally see in the mirror.*

Today I sit up out of bed and I'm still in the chair when Doug arrives. He's dropped Bek and Cal off at school and he's here for the day. *That's so fabulous!* The staff at the office can reach him on his mobile if need be. We talk, he reads the newspaper aloud, we eat a raspberry friand that he's brought in with a coffee, and he helps me back into bed for a sleep.

Dr Bradbury comes to visit. He's pleased with how I'm looking and how the operation went. It took a little longer than he anticipated, and the incision needed to be a little larger for the tumour and cyst to be removed in one piece. Now it's a matter of waiting for the pathology results, to determine my oncology treatment from here. He checks my dressing and asks how my pain levels are.

'Still uncomfortable, but getting better,' I reply. 'I haven't been using the pain relief via the intravenous drip as much today.'

With that being the case, the drip can come out and I can go onto oral pain relief.

It will free me up to have a shower in the morning and to walk around the ward a little. Step by step, I'm finding my way back!

In the afternoon Doug picks Bek and Cal up from school and they come in to see me. My bedside cabinet is cluttered with vases of native flowers. These have been sent from family and friends, and along with my yellow roses, my room is filled with colour and joy.

I look across at my family. We talk about their day. It's like a normal afternoon, only I'm sitting in a hospital bed and they're perched together on the other end. I smile and try to take in all they are saying, but my mind is so dulled from the pain relief and the distraction of my emotions is so strong, I find myself frequently wandering off.

To date this has been the hardest journey I've ever had to travel, and the fact that it may not be over yet pulls me away from the present. I'm living in limbo, waiting to hear the pathology results. I look back at them—they all make me smile. The strength and the laughter and love that they've brought to my hospital bed today completely envelopes me. And I know, that no matter what we will face in the next few days, with each other and with a handful of hope, we will find a way through.

*Chapter Seven*

# MY CANCER RECOVERY

*Swimming Further into the Ocean*

## APRIL 2007 – MARCH 2012

'Please, Heather,' my dear friend and neighbour, Jo Smith, pleads, holding me squarely by the shoulders and looking me straight in the eye. 'If there's one thing you ever do for me, it's that you get a second opinion.' Tears spill onto her cheeks and her voice begins to wobble. 'Only … one … thing … Heather …' she emphasises. 'You've got to see Professor Friedlander.' She draws me in and cradles me tight.

It's a late April afternoon and we're standing on the green grassy verge between our two houses. Only minutes earlier Doug and I had pulled into our driveway, fresh from our first consultation with my oncologist.

My head is spinning because I'm staring down the barrel of weeks and weeks of intensive chemotherapy, using a combination of hard-hitting drugs with all their possible, profound side effects: potential impaired vision and hearing, loss of balance, peripheral nerve damage. At present this is the conventional 'known' pathway of oncology care for Stage 1, Germ Cell Ovarian Tumours. It appears to be my only option right now, and I'm prepared to take it if I'm to be free from this deadly disease. It's just that what's shaking me up is the thought of losing my hearing like Dad, and being incapacitated in other ways. It's hitting me almost as hard as the cancer diagnosis itself.

But according to Jo, there might be another way. Her insistence is not based purely on emotion; it's from years of experience as an oncology nurse. She's currently working with a medical team who are at the cutting edge of cancer research and clinical trials here at the Prince of Wales Hospital.

'But what if it takes me ages to get an appointment?' I ask her. 'I don't have weeks to spare.'

'Here's the phone number. I'll let them know to expect your call and maybe there'll be a cancellation, which means you can slot straight in,' Jo replies.

So I phone them the next day and there's an appointment available next week. *I guess I should take it. I've got nothing to lose …*

A week later, I walk into a waiting room filled with women. Some women are with their partners and friends supporting them, others without. Some with hair, some without. Some with months to live, others without. They are all ages, degrees of illness and prognosis.

It affects me deeply. I'm living in a parallel universe where the words 'survival' and 'long life' are a rare commodity. No one talks about the weather or about people in glossy magazines, we talk about raw, real visceral stuff, such as Stage 2 and 3 and 4 cancer. And chemo, surgery, pain, families, dreams, goals to live until Christmas and birthdays and to the birth of grandchildren. There are some long-term and some very startling short-term scenarios.

The prognosis of the lady next to me is devastating: Stage 4. This is the worst stage of all. This means the cancer has spread to organs beyond her abdomen. It's no longer confined to the ovary, as in Stage 1, or only spread a limited way within the pelvis, like Stage 2, but it's moved beyond the lymph nodes and the lining of the abdomen, like Stage 3, and is spreading throughout her body. She has a young family. We've only met for five minutes, but we cry and we hug like we're childhood friends.

It's clear I'm sitting in a room full of warriors.

I hear my name and walk down the corridor and into the consulting room. Professor Michael Friedlander is a gentle man with a pair of wonderfully round-rimmed glasses and a disarming smile. I'm immediately at ease. We chat about my situation and the options. *Yes. Options!*

It just so happens he's aware of an alternative approach first published in medical papers from England. They've been successfully running a close surveillance program for my particular type of cancer, and for the stage that I'm at. What it involves are far more frequent physical examinations, CT scans and ultrasounds and blood tests than would normally accompany chemotherapy treatment, so that any cancer regrowth can be detected early.

It will extend over a period of five years. It's going to take a whole lot of time and commitment on my part, starting with hospital visits and tests every two weeks, which then slowly space out to monthly, then every second month and so on. But I'm up for that. Then if there's no sign of relapse in that period of five years, I'll be deemed to be cancer-free. Free to go!

The good news in all of this too, is that there is a back-up plan. If any of the tests reveal that the cancer has returned, then chemotherapy will be commenced straight away and the cure rate from this is known to be very high.

*That sounds logical. I like this approach.* What I also like about it is that it's a relatively new approach here in Australia, and I'll be helping shape the treatment for other women in the future.

I leave that consultation in a clear and positive mindset. I have a road map for the next stage of my journey through cancer, and I like that. *I love this structure. It feels so right.* I head home to give Jo a huge hug.

The surveillance program starts with fortnightly consul- tations, physical examinations, blood tests and scans, and through all of these, and then my monthly, and every second month visits, nothing shows up. With every passing day I feel like I'm steadily packing up my encounter with cancer, closing the door, and walking away. I feel incredibly grateful to be alive.

I'm back being a busy mum and wife and working hard at our business. Back being myself. The scar on my abdomen is healing. I can walk up stairs and drive again, and I'm regaining strength. Doug is an amazing cook and makes sure I'm eating well, and whenever we can, we go for long walks at the beach with Bek and Cal. I start on hormone replacement therapy, because my ovaries have been removed, and it keeps the symptoms of menopause at bay.

All is going well …

Until one morning when I wake with sharp abdominal pain. It's in my lower-right quadrant, right where my tumour had been. It persists throughout the day and I fear the worst—it must be growing back.

By the time Professor Friedlander sees me, I'm a pale, fragile, shaking mess. I'm more upset than the first time around. I don't want to be back there again.

As I sit opposite him at his desk, I desperately try to hold it together and not cry. But I don't, and I do. He reassures me and I settle down and he sends me off to have a CT scan.

Soon I'm back in that all too familiar backless, white, cotton hospital gown, laying motionless on the bed of the scanner. The machine whirrs and moves and clicks, and as it shifts me into the barrel, I'm taken back to the day of my diagnosis … back to fighting shadows of a monster I cannot see.

*What if they find another cancerous mass? Then what? What if I had my chance to fight it and I didn't. Should I have gone straight onto chemo?*

And then my surprisingly calm inner voice answers. *No regrets. You made the right decision. If the cancer has returned, then face it like the first time. Head on. With family and friends.*

I'll be as brave as I can be. Positive. Practical. Holding a handful of hope and raising a figurative fist to fight all the fear.

The CT scan is inconclusive. So I have an MRI scan. It picks up that I have a small amount of peritoneal fluid pooling in my abdominal cavity. It's perplexing, but fortunately there's no sign of a tumour.

My blood test for CA125 levels remains normal. A chest x-ray is clear too. Perhaps I have scar tissue, adhesions from surgery that are causing irritation, or perhaps it's a bowel infection.

But whatever it is, in a few days the terrible pain is gone and I pick myself up and carry on. *Phew!* I feel incredibly relieved to have dodged this possible bullet, and I tell myself that I'll do everything I can to be as healthy and as fit as possible.

Months pass, and then I'm into a new year—it's 2008. I begin to think less and less about what I've been through. It's only when I walk along the well-worn path back into the consulting rooms to receive my latest test results, and have physical check-ups, that it all comes flooding back.

Each time I hang on to every word Professor Friedlander says and hold my breath as he tells me the latest findings. I'm acutely aware there are two directions I can head out from here, and fortunately, the one I am on at this stage is leading me on the road to remission.

In January 2009, almost two years after surgery, I feel strong enough to do something completely new and different.

For several years now, Bek and Cal have been involved in the junior surf lifesaving program called Nippers at Coogee Beach. And while Doug has run the program, and became a surf lifesaver, I've been content to simply help out with activities on the sand.

With Cal in his final year of the program, he'll be graduating up to doing volunteer patrols with the senior club. That means we'll have a very big hole in our world, after nine years of Sunday mornings at the beach, and involved so closely with our friends at the surfclub; however, it also opens up a whole new opportunity for me—a chance to step up to become a surf lifesaver too.

So I sign up with some other mums to do my Surf Lifesaving Bronze Medallion. It's something I never imagined I would ever do. For one thing, I'm not an ocean swimmer. Growing up in the far-eastern suburbs of Melbourne, my family only went to the beach twice a year. When I say 'beach', it was to Seaford, a sheltered stretch of sand in Port Phillip Bay, nowhere near the wild ocean breakers on the back beaches of Bass Strait.

Then one Sunday morning, in late January, I find myself in my swimming cozzies looking out at the gentle waves at Coogee Beach. They are a brilliant blue. It's a perfect day, except for the water temperature, as it's a chilly 14°C, and I have a qualifying 400-metre swim to do.

I adjust my goggles for the umpteenth time and pull my swimming cap down over my ears. I check the ties of my two tone blue surf lifesaving cap. Here goes ... I'm going to give this a shot, along with twenty or so other brave and anxious mums and dads.

We're briefed on the course: swim from there, to there to there, which in my mind equates to swimming to New Zealand. The timekeeper says, 'Go!' We have nine minutes.

I wade out several steps, then porpoise under a couple of waves and start swimming freestyle out to sea. Within seconds my face is numb and the temperature of the water makes me breathless. I try to slow my breathing and get into a rhythm and press on. There's a red buoy to get to first.

Many of us reach it at the same time and the water churns wildly with our arms and legs. We turn south for 200 metres. Halfway into that, I resort to sidestroke to lift my face out from the chilly water. I need to regroup and catch my breath. But this is costing me serious time and I slip away from the back of the pack.

'Come on ... come on ...' I tell myself. 'You've got to put your face back into the sea and swim.'

So I take a deep breath and start freestyle again. I focus on counting my strokes to distract me from the cold and my growing fatigue. Finally I reach the second marker and aim back towards the shore. But with the tide going out I find myself going nowhere. I'm swimming in one spot. I begin to flounder and panic. Fortunately, a well-timed wave washes me in to the beach. I stand up and wobble out of the water.

Despite as wretched as I feel, it's all been worth it! I've done it in eight minutes something or other … and I've passed the first test.

Over the next eight weeks we have theory on wave types, rips, rescues, first aid, signals and resuscitation. There's cross-training fitness sessions at 6am every Tuesday and Thursday to improve our general fitness, which Doug leads, and practical sessions every Sunday to learn specific rescue techniques.

I honestly spend a whole lot more time hanging off the back of my comfort zone than staying within it. I'm diving under plunging waves, swimming way out of my depth, overcoming anxiety, trying to catch my breath when the ocean winds whip water in my face. But I stick with it, and start to see improvements. I'm gaining more confidence and steadily getting fitter, and although I've still got a long way to go, I'm proud of myself for starting out on this journey in the first place.

Another Sunday morning session finds me standing on the shoreline, clutching the black handles of my yellow rescue board. I'm 165 centimetres tall and 55 kilograms, and it seems as long and as heavy as a semitrailer.

I'm waiting, ready for my training cue: 'Rescue, rescue, rescue!'

*There it is.*

I race in to the water, and slide myself onto the board and start paddling. Luckily, I get through the oncoming wave before it breaks and I race out to sea. My friend, Tina Nixon, is my pretend patient, so I tell her I'm a lifesaver and that I'm here to help, and everything's going to be okay. I assist her onto the front of my board and we paddle back through the waves and into shore. *Done.*

March arrives and so does our Part A exam. We're tested on our theory and first aid scenarios. It's such a hot, humid evening and there's a thunderstorm brewing. We've divided into groups of eight and allocated an assessor to ask us questions and check out our CPR technique. Despite a few nerves, and a forehead glistening with perspiration, all the information in my head somehow manages to come out. I pass.

However, by the time the weekend of our Part B practical exam arrives, I've developed bronchitis. It's a telling sign I've been pushing myself too hard, my reserves are just not up to speed post-cancer.

*But I've come this far. I can't give up now. I'll give it my best shot, within reason that is.*

Sunday morning dawns a clear and beautiful day. Doug, Cal and I arrive at Maroubra Beach to meet everyone else, only to find the northerly swell has picked up. The waves are pounding the shore, and powerful flash rips are appearing in the churning foam. It's an understatement to say we're feeling a little anxious.

The decision by the chief assessor is to press ahead with the exam, as it will simply be adapted to the conditions. We'll do a 'run, swim, run' at the more sheltered northern section of the beach. Even so, it still looks like a washing machine.

We have eight minutes to do a 200-metre run in the soft sand, 200-metre swim and a 200-metre run in the sand to finish off. I line up with everyone at the start line in the sand. The chief assessor liaises with the timekeeper.

Cal and Doug wait in the waves with the rest of the water safety team, just in case we need assistance.

'Ready, set, go!'

I run the 200 metres in pretty good time and turn towards the sea. I pull my goggles over my eyes and turn my body sideways as a wave comes through. I do a couple of porpoise dives then launch into freestyle. Our 100-metre marker is one of the water safety guys treading water, holding a rescue tube up in the air. I lift my head every few strokes to catch sight of him and to stay on track.

It's a wash of waves and foam. I reach the marker. I'm halfway. I'm relieved and turn back towards shore. But I'm tiring quickly ... I'm breathless, the impact of my bronchitis is kicking in. I sidestroke for about 10 metres, and tell myself to stay calm, but I can feel the panic rising up inside.

I do my best to keep up with everyone, but my goggles are fogging and I'm slipping further behind. *How far have I got to go?* My feet still can't reach the sand. I'm swallowing water, my arms are weak and my body seems to weigh a ton as I haul it through the water. My swim stroke is all over the shop. I'm hitting the wall ...

Doug and Cal appear to my left and I call out anxiously to them, 'I don't think I can make it!' I'm so upset, exhausted, devastated and desperate to get back onto shore.

Doug replies, very calmly, 'Yes, you can, Heather. You know you can stand up there.'

'What?'

A wave washes me forward and my feet touch the sand. That sweet, sweet sand! It's a huge surprise and a relief!

I flop into a couple of porpoise dives and the next few waves help me stumble onto shore. Now it's a matter of shuffling my shattered body across the soft sand for the 200-metres to the finish line.

I make it in under eight minutes! It's a miracle. I've passed my run, swim, run. I celebrate by wandering off a little distance and throwing up in the sand.

All that's left to do is a tube rescue, a board rescue, a spinal injury retrieval from the water and some first aid scenarios.

We have a few minutes to regroup. My tube rescue goes well, and then up next is my board rescue. My 'patient' swims out about 100 metres, to beyond the wave zone. My assessor gives me the go ahead to go.

I grab my giant yellow rescue board and race into the waves. My heart is pounding and all I can hear is the crash of the surf. The surf conditions have eased slightly, but it's still like running into the danger zone. One wave breaks and pushes me back. A second makes me slip sideways off the board. I'm facing the power of the ocean head on. But I'm determined. I'm not here to be tossed about in the white wash. I've got to get repositioned and paddle out to my patient.

I slide myself back to the centre of my board just as a huge wave rises up in front. I flip upside down, into an eskimo roll to negotiate it, and hang on, but I'm no match for the power of the water. It pounds my board into my face and washes me to shore. I stand up a bloody mess. My teeth have cut through my lower lip and my chin and cheek are numb and swelling fast.

The assessor sends me straight to the surf lifesaving patrol tent a little way up the beach for first aid. I get there and they sit me down to check me out. They ask me if I've been in a fight. I tell them I have, with a wave. I press a piece of gauze to my lip to stop the bleeding and apply a bag of ice.

So here I am. Sitting alone. Knocked out of my bronze medallion exam … gutted …

I watch as my friends complete their board rescues and get ready to do spinal rescues.

Five minutes passes. My lip stops bleeding. *I can't just sit here. I've got to get back in and finish it off.* So I excuse myself and head back to the assessment. I reassure the assessor that I feel okay, even if I don't look it. She gives me the role of the patient for the spinal rescue and then I help with patient carries and we do some mock first aid scenarios on the sand—a heart attack and a hypothermic patient.

I've now done everything except for the board rescue—I'm so close to passing.

*Is it possible that I can give the board rescue one more shot?* My face may be battered, but my arms and legs have recovered enough to get me out there in the water.

I talk it over with the assessor and she allows me one more go. My friend, Veronica, swims out as my patient. I stand on the shoreline holding the black handle of my 'semitrailer', ready to go. I can feel the adrenaline surging through my body. My heart's racing and my legs are shaking as I watch the wind blow sea spray up from the waves.

Veronica puts up her hand to indicate she's ready for 'rescue', and my assessor says, 'Go! Good luck, Heather!'

I time my entry into the water much better this time. A wave has just broken and if I'm quick enough to get onto the board and paddle strongly, I'll race over the top of the next one before it breaks. I paddle like I've never paddled before.

My lip is throbbing and water splashes into my face. I use every ounce of strength to get me through the wave zone, to get to the calmer water, and to Veronica, and I do!

I am so happy and relieved. I fight to keep my tears at bay. I'm totally breathless and spent. I help her climb on the board as best I can and we position ourselves to paddle back.

All we have to do now is get back to the beach without getting knocked off. My arms feel like empty pipes, but with Veronica paddling too, we skim across the water. There's a wave looming behind us so we slow and let it roll through to break in front of us.

*Okay, it's time to go. We've got to beat the other one so that it breaks behind us and not on us. Paddle, paddle. It's rising up. Come on arms … come on!*

I hear it break and we feel its power boost our board forward. The foam and wash spills onto our legs and we hang on for dear life as we're carried on a bumpy ride all the way into shore. Doug retrieves my board, while I help my 'patient' up to the dry sand. I give her the biggest hug. Because of her, I've done it!

Our group huddles together and we have a debrief and celebratory hugs. We turn our lifesaving caps inside out, from our Coogee two blue colours, to the red and yellow quartered side, and tie them exuberantly under our chins. My assessor comes up beside me and tells me she's impressed by my determination.

I smile and thank her for the opportunity to have another go. 'It's about never giving up, isn't it,' I tell her, 'no matter what we face.'

She nods and walks away.

Doug and Cal hug me tightly and wrap me up in my towel. Today, I am a brand-new surf lifesaver.

A few days later, I find myself back as a cancer patient. I'm back at the Prince of Wales Hospital to get the results for my next six-monthly blood tests and ultrasound. I tell Professor Friedlander that I'm a lifesaver. He's very impressed but looks at my swollen lip with a little concern. 'You certainly earned it!'

'Who would have thought I'd be doing anything like this when I first came to see you two years ago!' I blurt.

My results are clear. He beams at me and tells me it makes his day being able to give someone positive news. I understand where he's coming from.

Sadly, there are several women that I don't get to see again—they don't make it—there are empty chairs in the waiting room that soon fill up with new women. It's devastating to see. *I need to do something. I need to help somehow.*

Time tumbles by. Life's generally busy. Bek and Cal go on overseas exchanges with school. I do surf lifesaving patrols at the beach. I even do my first rescue, an eight-year-old girl caught in a rip.

Then my five-year anniversary arrives. It's March 2012. The medical surveillance program is complete. From here on I'll only need to see my gynaecologist every six months for the CA125 blood tests and pap smears.

I don't come to this appointment prepared to say goodbye to Professor Friedlander, as I didn't realise it was going to be my last. I choke up with emotion. The care and compassion that he and all the staff have given me here has been absolutely life-changing, and life-saving.

Understandably, I'm reluctant to go. But I know that the door back to normal life is open and I will take my first few tentative steps on my own. It's time to close this chapter and walk out into the sunshine. I'm a survivor. I'm a positive statistic that will help shift the balance against this devastating disease.

It's now time to reset my compass—to point my feet in the direction of living life to the full and go. I tell myself, 'I'm going to amp it up from here!'

*Chapter Eight*

# MY RUNNING JOURNEY

## *Starting at the Very Beginning*

## 2012 – 2015

April 2012 …

'Hey everyone, I've got a great idea!' I say enthusiastically, putting a forkful of peas in my mouth, '… and I've been wanting to do it for years.'

Bek, Cal and Doug look up from their dinner plates, wondering what on earth I'm about to say.

'Why don't we sign up to run the 4-kilometre Mother's Day Classic?'

I may as well have said I was going to dye my hair pink, gauging by their reactions. Me? Run? I hadn't run any real distance since primary school.

'It's for a great cause,' I add, sounding like a salesperson. 'We'll be raising funds for breast cancer research and it will help women just like Grandma Elsie and Aunty Christine.'

I don't need to say anymore—they're in.

After dinner, and with a cup of tea in hand, we sit down to register online. I tick the boxes, pay the fees and arrange for our race bibs, pink hats, T-shirts and socks to be posted out. *Perfect. Done.*

So this is our plan—Bek, Cal and I will get out there and train every day, and Doug will be our support crew. He'd love to run but unfortunately he's had past injuries to his knees.

The following afternoon, Bek and Cal wait patiently downstairs while I rummage in my wardrobe. I'm becoming increasingly flustered. *There's got to be something in here I can wear.* I don't own any lycra or leggings, or sports shorts. The only option I can find is a baggy old pair of gardening shorts and my faded blue and white striped T-shirt. *This will have to do.*

I wriggle into a pair of ancient, stiff, white runners, and then I grab the car keys and we go.

At Centennial Park, Cal takes Bek and I through some warm-up stretches. I'm alarmingly inflexible and my toes seem to be much further away than yesterday. Next, we stand beneath the canopy of a magnificent fig tree and go over our training plan together.

Bek and Cal are clear on what they need to do, they've run 6-kilometre cross-country events at high school before, but for me it's daunting and brand-new. Apart from running short distances in the soft sand at the beach for surf lifesaving, I've never run a distance like this in my life.

Today our plan is to run one full lap, clockwise, on the bitumen pathway. That's 3.6 kilometres in total. Starting with a slow jog for about 200 metres, we'll then pick it up from there. If we're tired, we can walk, or if we're exhausted, we can cut back across the park between the duck ponds.

Sounds like a good solid plan.

The afternoon sun shines warmly on our backs as we set off. We jog shoulder to shoulder, and then at the 200-metre mark we pick up the pace. Cal's long legs carry him effortlessly along. Soon he's metres ahead. Bek stays steadily by my side. She talks me along in encouraging bursts.

At the 500-metre mark I spot a water bubbler. *Perfect.* I'm already feeling breathless and hot in the face. I stop and have a sip. From here it's up a slight hill, over a side road and back beneath the magnificent fig trees.

At the 1-kilometre mark, my thigh muscles are so weak and stiff that my pace slows dramatically. Up ahead there's another water bubbler, and I point it out happily to Bek. It's a good excuse to stop.

By now Cal is a dot in the distance, and I don't want to even think about how far we have to go. Lycra-clad cyclists whizz past us on their circuits as I leave the sanctuary of the bubbler and shuffle on.

'You're going really well!' Bek chirps with encouragement as we run across Parkes Drive.

'Thanks, Bek,' I say, but inside I feel otherwise.

My bulky shorts are weighing me down and my T-shirt's glued to my back. I'm light-headed to the point of seeing stars. 'I think I'll sit down on these sandstones for a moment,' I say, slowing to a walk and moving to the side of the path. I ease down to put my spinning head in my hands.

This is far tougher than I expected. I should have snacked on something before I ran ... but right now I don't have a clue about race nutrition.

Bek puts a concerned arm around me and I honestly feel like crying, but I stop myself short. I have to keep on going. We're running for Grandma Elsie and Auntie Christine, and for all those other women out there who've battled breast cancer. Such beautiful souls taken from us all, far too soon.

What I'm going through right now is absolutely nothing compared to what they've endured, so if I can see this run through, stand myself at the start line of the Mother's Day Classic, and do something to help them in my own little way, then I'll be incredibly happy. Determination flickers inside. I wipe my face on my T-shirt and stand up to start running again.

We pass the busy children's cycleway, skirt around the corner near Busbys Pond and into the final kilometre. It's slightly up hill, but that's not going to stop me. Cal reappears to check on how we are. Then just as we started, we jog the final 200 metres, side by side.

The next afternoon we're back at the park. I run past the first water bubbler, but when I reach the 2-kilometre mark, my stiff concrete legs and the dizzy stars reappear. I walk for 50 metres, then pick it up again and run all the way to the end.

From here we have two and a half weeks until Mother's Day.

The following afternoon, Bek and I shop for new runners. There's a choice of blue or pink. It's a no-brainer. Pink is perfect for the Mother's Day Classic. I also try on a pair of mid-thigh length lycra leggings. They feel very aerodynamic and I model a few running poses in the change rooms and laugh out loud. *Am I brave enough to wear these? Yes, I am!* When I get home I put away my old gardening shorts and shoes.

A few days later our race bibs and event T-shirts, caps and socks arrive in the mail. Everything's so pink. It's fabulous!

May 2012 …

Saturday morning Bek, Cal and I mix things up and run anti-clockwise around the park. I run with a water bottle in my hand to avoid stopping at the bubblers. I take frequent, clumsy sips, but this time I make it all the way around without stopping. It's a breakthrough! Doug brings Rusty, our dog, for a walk and is impressed with our progress.

The next week we add the missing 400 metres to make it 4 kilometres. I run it in one go. I surprise myself. I'm definitely feeling stronger. It's taken me two full weeks to get to this stage.

Another week of training and I focus on my speed. I buy pink running watches for us, and discover that I can run 1 kilometre in exactly 5 minutes 27 seconds. My legs still get tired towards the end, but they're not what they used to be. I can see other improvements too—Cal's no longer a dot in the distance, I don't see stars, and Bek and I can actually talk the whole way around.

We keep up the training most days and very soon it's Saturday, the day before Mother's Day. We don't run—we have a rest day. It feels so strange.

There's no room in my head for anything else. I can't wait until tomorrow. We have spaghetti bolognese for dinner, because I've read somewhere that pasta is great the night before a race. I lay all my running gear out on my bedside table. My race bib is pinned to my pink T-shirt. Mother's Day Classic, here I come!

Mother's Day 2012 …

It's a gorgeous sunny, blue-sky morning. There are road closures for the run, so Doug drops us off in Woolloomooloo and arranges to pick us up from here in three hours time. We climb the old sandstone stairs behind the Art Gallery of NSW, and cross the road into the grassy Domain. It's just on 7am, but already there's a growing crowd decked out in pink: pink wigs, pink tule tutus, and bright pink lipstick. We fit right in.

In the middle of the field they've set up a tribute wall to remember those lost to breast cancer. I pin up our handwritten card in memory of Grandma Elsie and Auntie Christine.

Emotions are running high. Bek, Cal and I stand together and hug, and I whisper to myself, 'Every centimetre of this race is for you, Elsie and Christine.'

A wild zumba warm-up puts us through our paces, and then it's time to walk to the start line. We're swept along in a sea of fuchsia as it funnels onto Macquarie Street. This is my first experience of being in a pre-race crush, it's so up close and personal, and I hear a lot of laughter and nervous chatter.

I'm excited to be here, but at the same time, a little anxious. *How will I go? Will I make it all the way to the finish line? How steep are those hills? How many drink stations will there be? Are there any water bubblers?*

I'm not very sure about any of the above, but what I am sure of, is that I'll do my very best to run the whole 4 kilometres in one go.

Disco music pumps, the countdown to the race begins—ten, nine, eight … three, two, one … The hooter sounds and we're off! I fling my arms up. *Woohoo!* The race is on and little do I know as I step forward over the timing mat, that I'm running into a whole new world.

It's a shuffling start, but after the first corner, space soon clears for my feet. Cal wishes Bek and I good luck and takes off like a rocket. The next time we'll see him is under a tree beyond the finish line.

Bek and I run together, smiling, swimming in a sea of harmony and pastels. *This is such great fun.* We run past the impressive sandstone columns of the Art Gallery and then fly down a hill. Before we know it we're pacing past Boy Charlton Pool, where people are knocking out their methodical laps. We curve around Mrs Macquarie's Chair, and all the cups and clutter and the chatter of the drinks station.

I catch glimpses of the harbour and it's such a soul-lifting sight … and suddenly something clicks inside. It's a flash of clarity, a moment of truth—I've discovered, at last, after all these years, that I really, really do love long-distance running!

I pick up my pace, there's no stopping me now, and I've got a Mother's Day smile pegged all across my face. There's 100 metres to go. It's a magnificent stretch, beneath two grand lines of towering fig trees. Bek and I sprint all the way and cross beneath the finish line gantry holding hands. *We've done it!*

We give each other an enormous, sweaty hug.

A few minutes later we locate Cal leaning against the trunk of a tree and slide down to sit next to him, to eat apples and chat.

'I'm having the most awesome Mother's Day,' I tell them, 'and this beats breakfast in bed!'

As we walk back to meet Doug in the designated place, I think about how this race has been a brand-new experience for our family. It's given us an opportunity to do something tangible to help the lives of other grandmas and aunties, and the privilege of honouring our own. And even though it's over, this is just the beginning …

Over dinner, later that week, something similar happens again.

'Hey, I've got a great idea everyone, and it's something I've been wanting to do for years.'

Bek, Cal and Doug look across the dinner table at me, wondering what I'm talking about now.

'Why don't we sign up to do the City2Surf? It's 14 kilo-metres from Hyde Park to Bondi Beach.'

But this time they're not surprised. It's achievable now.

The next three months we build up to that distance and we run it together. A few days after that, we sign up for the Blackmores Sydney Half Marathon, which is 21.0975 kilometres.

And so the story goes ... with every race that we register for, it's a step up in distance, and challenge, and it gives me another opportunity to celebrate being a survivor. Every day I'm feeling stronger and I gain so much joy by simply putting on my running shoes and going for a run.

I begin to research race nutrition, and learn about gels and electrolyte drinks and what to eat pre- and post-race. I start using terminology like 'carbo loading' and 'tapering'. I create training schedules for each race and I stick to them diligently. Some days Bek, Cal and I train together, other days we run alone.

We vary the routes to keep thing interesting. I love running the coastal path to South Bondi and back, especially in the morning, to see the sun shake itself free from the ocean. Other days we do the circuits at Centennial Park, or do cross-training in the sand and the waves at Coogee Beach.

This all works well.

There are definitely days when I struggle out of bed, when I'm tired or it's rainy and cold. But I lace up my shoes and get out there and I'm glad that I do. My fitness grows and I steadily build the kilometres in my legs.

Soon it's time to buy a new pair of shoes and running singlets. Even Christmas gifts become running-related. Bek and Cal give me a pair of lime-green running shorts—they're not going to lose me in a hurry!

The new year arrives—it's 2013. I sign up for a number of races: the Mother's Day Classic (4 kilometres), the SMH Half Marathon (21 kilometres) and the City2Surf (14 kilometres).

Then I take things up a giant notch.

On the 22 of September, Cal and I attempt our first full marathon, the Blackmores Sydney Marathon, which is 42.195 kilometres. It's a daunting task, but I focus on one day at a time.

I research training schedules and print one out and put it on the desk at home. I tick the days and distances off as I go, and Cal joins me when he can. He's studying year twelve at school, so he runs whenever he gets a chance.

We train at Centennial Park, running clockwise laps just like we did for the Mother's Day Classic. Then we gradually build up to 25 kilometres then 28 kilometres. Cal has exams, so I do a training run alone of 32 kilometres. I keep passing the place where I sat on the sandstones with my head in my hands on that first training run. It's hard to believe that was only eighteen months ago.

The night before the race, I lay all my running gear out on my bedside table. My race bib is pinned on, ready to go. I have gels, lolly snakes and an old jumper that I'll wear then donate at the start line.

This race is for my mum and dad. My rocks, my dearest friends, and the original adventurous spirits in my world. Tomorrow I'll run every single step in honour of them.

It's a really cold morning and Doug drives Cal and I to Central Station to catch the train to Milsons Point. We race onto the platform to get the next service and our carriage quickly fills with lean legs and running shoes. We rattle and sway across the Sydney Harbour Bridge, and the sun flashes in through the windows. Everyone disembarks at the next station.

Cal and I do our best to stay warm and wait patiently in the portaloo queue. We do a few stretches, drink water, take a couple of photos and move into our starting corral. I peel off my jumper and throw it to the side for collection.

Because Cal and I run at such different paces, we agree to meet each other at the end of the race. We hug, and then the starter gun sounds. We're off. I turn my music on as Cal disappears ahead. The road turns sharply and takes me up onto the bridge. People have replaced cars, so I choose lane number three. A city-bound train rattles by and the distinctive grey metal arches, with their fist-like rivets, stretch high above me to the sky.

Before I know it I'm curling through the sandstone corkscrew and emerging onto the Cahill Expressway. *Wow!* The city buildings and Circular Quay are right beside me.

A few people overtake me, but I resist the urge to chase them down. I'm staying true to my original race plan to keep the four-hour pacesetter and his flag within reach.

I spin around Mrs Macquarie's Chair, through Hyde Park and up Oxford Street. The race leaders are heading back towards the city already. *Incredible. I'm not even halfway through!* I reach the football stadium and my heart sinks. Cal is standing to the side of the road looking for me. Something's wrong …

It's his Achilles tendon. We run slowly together for another kilometre to get to the first aid station in Centennial Park. I sit him down and bandage it up, then we press on for another kilometre, but by the 26th kilometre, it's far too painful for him to go on.

He's absolutely gutted, and so am I.

I call Doug, he's only five minutes away, so he'll pick Cal up soon. I sit down to wait, but Cal insists, 'Madre, you need to keep going!'

'But I don't want to leave you,' I respond.

'No, you need to go. You need to finish your race and while you're at it, finish it for me.'

I give Cal a hug and I promise I will.

The kilometres tick over and I try desperately to catch up with the four-hour pacesetter and his flag, but he's slipped away somewhere along Anzac Parade. It's a huge mental blow, but unexpected things have happened, and I have to let it go. I need to be adaptable and stay positive because that's what's going to get me through this marathon today.

I set myself a new challenge to stay in front of the 04:15 pacesetter, and I refocus on my mum and dad, and Cal …

I run back down Oxford Street and the gradient makes my calves stiffen, so I slow my pace and push on. I take another glucose gel and have an electrolyte drink at the next aid station and throw a cup of water all over my core. The 32-kilometre marker appears on the left. This is the furthest I've ever run in training, so as I pass this flag, I'm on new ground.

The course weaves around the back buildings of Pyrmont, then across a steep, sweeping flyover from Darling Harbour. The sun is out. It's exposed and challenging. My legs are aching, and I'm light-headed.

'Come on … hang in there, I don't want to see stars!' I tell myself.

I finally shake myself free from the never-ending Hickson Road and turn under the Harbour Bridge to see the Opera House sails rising out of the harbour.

*That's the finish line just over there. All I need to do is get through Circular Quay and it's over!*

A race photographer appears on the right. I smile, stride out and pretend I'm okay, and then as soon as he's out of sight I let my shoulders slump down.

Then I'm onto the pavement leading to the Opera House. Emotion wells up inside me. *Mum, Dad, Cal, this is for you!*

The crowd cheers. I find a second wind, and sprint across the line! I've finished it in 04:11:40, somehow managing to stay ahead of that looming 04:15 pacesetter.

The recovery area beneath the Opera House steps is a concrete oasis. I sit there for quite some time studying my finisher's medal and absentmindedly eating an apple. I'm exhausted. I watch as other runners hobble in and give them a smile.

*What a day! What a memorable day. I honestly can't believe I've run a full marathon.* It was more like a whole 42.195 kilometres of aching limbs, sheer grit and determination. That same determination I'd plugged into when I was fighting cancer and I needed to revisit it today to get myself across the finish line.

This race pushed me past my mental, emotional and physical limits, further than I have ever pushed myself before. It was far tougher than anticipated. But the incredible joy and relief, and sense of achievement that I felt right now, and that I'd done it for Mum and Dad and Cal, had definitely made it all worth it.

When I do eventually move, it's a long, agonisingly 400-metre wobble to the wharf to catch a ferry to Rose Bay. Doug picks me up from the other end and whisks me away home.

Over the next few weeks, Cal's Achilles tendon recovers well and we promise each other that one day we'll run another marathon together. *I'm looking forward to that day.*

A couple of months later I run the Marysville Half Trail Marathon to raise funds for the 2009 bushfire appeal. It's great to see the little town and the blackened forest coming back to life again. The course follows the same logging trails that we explored in our old station wagon at Easter in the 1970s. My head and heart are brimming with memories and emotion the whole way along.

Before I know it, 2014 arrives and I fill it with even more races, including the Mother's Day Classic, but this time Bek, Cal and I choose to run the 8-kilometre race. I'm so excited to see how far I've come, and happily surprised at how my body is holding up.

Even after two years, the joy of running isn't fading, in fact it's growing and it keeps me training almost every single day and distracted thinking about the next challenge. Despite mostly running alone now, I know I'm not running in isolation. I couldn't be doing this without the support of Doug, Bek and Cal. I'm so incredibly grateful.

I run the Canberra Full Marathon, and Doug and I have a mini holiday together. I learn some very big lessons with this race. I go out way too fast, to find myself fading desperately at the 25-kilometre mark. I also strain my Iliotibial band because of the steep camber of the road. By the time 32 kilometres arrives, I'm running like a pirate and almost swearing like one too.

It's a picturesque course around Lake Burley Griffin, but it's one of the hardest marathon experiences I've ever had. It takes a frustrating six weeks for my ITB to recover.

The other races I run include the SMH Half Marathon; Centennial Park Ultra (50 kilometres); Blackmores Sydney Full Marathon; Melbourne Full Marathon; and the Marysville Full Trail Marathon.

And it's this year that I hear about a marathon in the Antarctic …

'What do you mean they run marathons in Antarctica?' I turn and ask my friend Bram Cassidy as we shuffle past the hallowed stands of the MCG in the crush of a crowd. We're on our way to the start line of the Melbourne Marathon. The air is chilly, filled with expectation, as well as an overpowering aroma of Dencorub.

Bram smiles back at me and nods confirmation.

'Wow!' I blurt loudly. 'That's a really gallant and adventurous thing to do!'

I can't remember how this topic even dropped into our pre-race conversation, but from that moment on, my head is in the clouds. All I want to do is get to the start line, get to the finish line and get back to my hotel room to search online for 'marathons run on ice'.

Bram and I funnel across a footbridge above the railway tracks, then hug goodbye and seek out our start groups. I squeeze in through the barriers and stretch and jog enthusiastically on the spot with my thousand or so new-found friends. I'm still so sidetracked from my imminent race that I forget to take my pre-race energy gel.

It's the 12 October 2014.

Suddenly, the starter gun sounds and I fly off down Flinders Street with every scrap of good sense still off in the land of icebergs and penguins. I push hard around Albert Park Lake, stride out along St Kilda Esplanade, race past the pier where Dad proposed to Mum, and skirt the wooden, stomach-churning rollercoaster of Luna Park.

Somewhere out along the course I look down at my blue running shoes pounding the bitumen, and wonder what it would be like to run in snow. It would be very different to this, that's for sure, as sweat drips from my forehead onto my singlet below.

At the 21-kilometre mark my fingers start to swell. I'm heating up, and my body is stressing out. I am pushing myself way too hard. I squeeze an energy gel into my mouth and sip cool water from an aid station. I toss the remainder of the cup across my core. I am now in damage control, my race plan totally in tatters.

Back onto Alexander Parade, I climb into the hilly section of the Botanical Gardens, and there, in among all those beautiful spring garden beds, I hit that dreaded 'wall'. Lightheaded, nauseous, and with legs as heavy as lead, it is down to two things to get me through—the songs of Midnight Oil and some single-minded, soul-grinding willpower.

Finally I am out of the gardens and puffing across the Princes Bridge. The MCG comes back into view. Only one more kilometre to go and my race will be finished.

Over tram tracks … Under flashing traffic lights … Up the chute … At last it is done. Three hours 58 minutes.

I seek refuge in some shifting shade, just beyond the finish line. I could stay here forever, but no, I pull myself up. I have work to do, as there's something I need to look up on the internet!

Eight-hundred metres seems like an endless plank when you're walking like a pirate. I hobble along the footpath, swept along in a sea of exhausted, but euphoric individuals. There are bursts of laughter on my left, which balance out the philo- sophical race post-mortems on my right. On everyone's chests the marathon medals swing like hypnotic silver pendulums. Left, right, left, right.

I negotiate a gutter and peel off into the foyer of my hotel. An empathetic doorman takes one look at me and promptly presses the button to call the lift. I nod gratefully and say thank you, then stand and wait. There's no escaping my reflection in the mirrored lift door, it's so telling—my face is flushed, and my skin so encrusted with sweat, I look more like a pink Himalayan salt shaker than a living, breathing human being.

Ten minutes later, and courtesy of very efficient room service, I have two large bags of ice firmly planted on my knees and a bottle of chilled apple juice in my hand. I reach for my laptop. This is the moment I've been running all morning for. I type in two words, with my puffy forefingers: Antarctic Marathon.

Bam! Up comes the 'Ice Marathon'. Bram was right!

I click on the website, which states: 'The Ice Marathon is a race held every year on the Union Glacier near the Ellsworth Mountain Range in Antarctica.'

'Wow!' I lean in closer and read on.

'The next race is scheduled for November 2014.'

'That's next month!' I conclude very cleverly.

I send off an enquiry and a reply comes back within minutes—'We're so sorry, this race is already full, but please keep in touch for next year.'

Okay …

I shower and put on my favourite retro flower dress and head downstairs to the hotel restaurant—it's as far as my legs will let me orbit right now. As the lift door opens into the lobby, the doorman is quick to tell me I look a whole lot better. I say thank you and nod gratefully.

I order a hamburger and a side of fries, and hungrily settle into my chair. Out the window the river of runners and medals continues to flow past.

I've learnt a great deal from my race today—about what to do, what not to do—and that most importantly, when it comes to the crunch, that willpower and music, can get you through. I contemplate what my next run will be—perhaps the Sixfoot Track Marathon in March?

But deep inside, the idea of running on ice keeps on bubbling away …

Two days later, I'm home. Doug asks me, 'How does Paris sound?'

'Sounds absolutely perfect!' I reply.

So it's decided then, the 'City of Lights' will be where we celebrate our 25th wedding anniversary and my 50th birthday!

While Doug looks up flights and accommodation, I wander off to my laptop to check the date of the Paris Marathon. *Yes, it works in with our schedule!* I make a mental note to book that soon.

A few days pass, we book flights and accommodation, and I sit down to register for the Paris Marathon. It's full. *No way!* I'm so disappointed, and there's a very strong sense of deja vu!

*Maybe there's another marathon in Europe at that time.* I do another search. Yes, there is … it's a little further north and perhaps a little cooler than Paris. It's the sister race of the Antarctic Marathon. It's The North Pole Marathon!

'Doug, how's this for an idea!' I call out from the kitchen table. The enthusiasm in my voice is a clear give away. I'm really eager to do this marathon.

I fill him in on what I've found.

'That could work,' he says, happy to go along with my plans.

I send off an enquiry, hoping and praying …

I receive a reply.

*I'm in!*

However, before I hit the ice, running, I say hello to 2015 by competing in the Sixfoot Track Marathon, in the Blue Mountains, which is 45 kilometres of rollercoaster running. I sign up with a good friend, Garren Constable, and it lives up to its reputation—phenomenal but punishing. There's no easing our way into it on the day.

As soon as the starter gun sounds, we're descending hundreds of stairs deep into the cradle of the Megalong Valley, climbing over styles between paddocks, fording the Coxs River and then surviving the uphill grind of the infamous pluviometer. I drink soft drink at every aid station and use up all my race gels.

The absolute relief and exhilaration when Garren and I hear those signature cowbells ringing, brings us racing off the trail and over the finish line.

Now it's time to turn my face to the north, completely north—to the very top of the world!

# Chapter Nine

# THE NORTH POLE MARATHON

## *The Run of a Lifetime*

## 2015

So how exactly do you train for a marathon at the North Pole, when it's the height of summer in Australia, and there's not a flake of snow to be found in Sydney?

It's January 2015, and the marathon is only three months away. I need to think fast.

I look into hiring an industrial freezer, but that seems a complicated exercise, and the idea of running on a treadmill in one doesn't really appeal to me at all.

So I go to the beach and run in the soft sand—ingenious! It's a similar action to running in soft snow, but it has the added bonus that if I get too hot, I can go for a swim.

As well as the beach, I include some longer runs, mainly at Centennial Park, just as if I was training for a normal road marathon.

*So what running gear do I need?* I check through the recommended website list. I head out shopping for thermal tops and leggings, a thermal singlet and underwear, a pair of waterproof, windproof and super warm mitts and liners, a woolly beanie and woolly merino socks with liners. I buy a black wind shell jacket with a faux fur lining on the hood (practical, but with a little bit of class!), and a balaclava (no class at all!).

The last thing I need are a pair of ski goggles. So I go shopping in town.

'Are you going skiing somewhere?' the shop assistant asks me in a fairly unenthusiastic voice and hands me a pair of goggles to try on.

It's a question he's probably asked a thousand customers before. 'No, I'm running a marathon at the North Pole,' I reply matter-of-factly, and pull the goggles down over my face.

There's complete silence. I sneak a sideways look at him. He looks perplexed. It's obvious he's trying to figure me out—am I being funny, am I completely mad, or is there the very slim chance that I might actually be telling the truth?

I give him an impish grin and five minutes later after a great conversation, he sells me the ski goggles at a discounted price!

I keep training hard—four mornings at the beach, one morning on the hills along the coastal walk from Coogee to Bondi, and another morning on the outside circuit at Centennial Park.

I buy a pair of trail runners and break these in. They're water-resistant, comfortable, and have amazing grip on the sole—perfect for the snow.

I keep a running diary that tracks my training, and I make a list of who I'm dedicating the 12 laps of the marathon to. I trial my ski goggles running along at the beach. They're comfortable, but they look hilarious, so out of place with my running gear. I half expect to see that ski shop assistant here—it would certainly confirm his suspicions I was mad.

The weeks race by. I prepare as best as I can. Then all I have to do is pack my bags, and go!

So with Doug and TG the Bear, we board the plane for Paris. It's the 28 March 2015. What a morning!

Paris is everything we'd imagined it to be—cobblestone streets, grand architecture, rich hot chocolates and buttery croissants. We walk and walk, and explore the city for hours on end. We find cafés and churches and bridges to cross, spring gardens and streetscapes to lose ourselves in. We visit the Arc de Triumph and The Louvre. We're immersed and enriched. Paris truly captures our hearts.

We begin our 25th wedding anniversary at sunrise with a 5-kilometre walk together in the Jardin des Tuileries. It's the 31 March 2015.

The air is fresh, the fountains are flowing and the bare spring branches are beginning to bud. We stop and sit next to a duck pond to reminisce about our wedding day. I remember Doug looked so handsome in his crisp white jacket and he remembers my incredibly curly hair and my elegant lacy high-necked dress. I still can't believe that was twenty-five years ago.

As we make our way back to the hotel a fine misty rain begins to fall. The concierge wishes us a happy anniversary and offers us umbrellas for the day. We visit the magnificent church of Mont Martre. It's so busy in here, yet so serene. The paintings on the ceilings are incredible.

We explore a winding laneway back down the mountain, and find a little café. Its menu is bursting with delicious soups, casseroles and pastries, and there are shelves and baskets overflowing with fresh produce. We sit at the window and eat and watch the world go by.

We wander into Tiffany & Co and buy matching rings to remind us of our vows, and Doug buys me a beautiful necklace with a signature key, for my upcoming birthday.

On my phone I've saved a copy of a photo that my dad took in Paris in 1969. It's a family pic, taken in front of the Eiffel Tower when we were heading home to Australia, from Canada. Doug and I set off to search for the exact location. We count the paths and garden beds and keep referencing back to the Eiffel Tower, then back to the photo.

At the corner of one particular garden bed we stop and look at each other. 'This is it!'

Suddenly we've peeled away all those years, back to when I was four years old, back with my family. Tears well up in my eyes. Doug takes my photo and gives me a hug. We hold hands and walk back along the Seine, and back into the present.

The next day we visit the Western front and wander through the rolling fields of Pozieres. I listen to our guide, but very soon all I can hear is my pounding heart. I drop back a little from the group. I need some time alone.

I turn around slowly and wonder how a place like this can cradle two such extremes. Today it's peaceful and green, and yet in the days of war it was filled with chaos and mud, chilled with death and fear. How did my two gentle-natured Australian grandfathers survive this horror? They were young men, serving in their battalions, following orders, climbing out of trenches and running over ridge lines into the tangle of wire and hellfire of no-man's-land. They fought for their lives, for the lives of their mates and for their country so far, far away. I can't even comprehend how my grandfather must have felt when he received news that his brother Stanley was lost.

In the village of Pozieres, the church bells chime and their song is carried out on a gentle wind. It lingers high in the trees. Not far from here is an Australian war cemetery. A close military friend of ours, Kel Pearce, has told us that my grandfather's brother, great Uncle Stanley, is buried here. I search through the well-worn register at the entrance gate to get the coordinates of his grave. There are pages and pages of names.

I set off among the plots, counting the rows, pausing to read inscriptions etched into the solemn, white headstones. A local groundsman is tending to the grass around Stanley's grave. He greets me with a gentle 'Bonjour' as I approach. I thank him for his care and shake his hand. I want to say so much more but my tears get in the way. We stand in silence for a moment or two, and then he nods respectfully and moves away to tend to another grave. I kneel and lay fresh poppies and gum leaves beneath his name.

'Thank you, Stanley, for your sacrifice. You've fallen so far away from family, but we'll carry you home in our hearts.'

It's a very quiet drive back through the farms, back to the busy streets of Paris.

A couple of days later I turn fifty! It's the 3 April. I'm officially half a century, as my dad would say. I celebrate with an early morning run along the Champs-Elysées and a breakfast of croissants and coffee. The first of many for the day!

I wear my key necklace and start to think about the upcoming days. They're counting down quickly to the North Pole Marathon.

On the 5 April, we pack our bags and head to Charles de Gaulle Airport. *This is so exciting. This next adventure is beginning!*

We board our flight to Oslo and it arrives mid-evening. Doug and I check into our hotel room and wander down to the bar to find some food. I look across the room to a group chatting together. I recognise one of them—it's the North Pole Marathon race director, Richard Donovan. He's here with his team and a handful of other competitors, who've flown in this evening too. *Fantastic!*

We sit together and eat and chat. Everyone's in great spirits and news is that the conditions at the North Pole are looking good.

The next day we're at the airport early. We check-in for our flight and proceed to the gate. I study the faces of the people milling around. I wonder who else is running the marathon. There are several lean men, whom I'm guessing are runners, then one appears who's an obvious choice—it's Annie Rawlinson. She's dressed as a polar bear!

As we board the plane, I catch the eye of Rob de Castella and Adrian Dodson-Shaw. I introduce myself briefly—what a privilege it is to shake their hands. Adrian Dodson-Shaw is an Indigenous marathon runner from Broome. It's going to be his second marathon but his first time ever in the snow. Rob de Castella, an Aussie icon, world champion marathon runner and all round good guy, is here as his mentor and friend. *Wow,* I think to myself as I wriggle into my window seat, *this is going to be an even more amazing experience!*

We take off.

The flight to Svalbard, Longyearbyen, is so scenic. Beneath our wings, dense fir forests and mountains give way to ice and snow. Every time I look out the window it's like I've turned a page in a National Geographic magazine. I spend some time writing in my diary and thinking.

We have a quick stop off at Tromso, disembark, do the circuit through customs, and then we're back in the air, heading North. I have a little snooze. It's a one hour forty minute flight.

The seatbelt sign illuminates. We begin our descent and circle above the runway at Longyearbyen. I can see the icy sea, a pocket full of colourful cottages, and snow on the surrounding hills.

Doug and I look at each other—are we really about to land in the northern most town in Norway?

There's a taxidermied polar bear in the middle of the baggage carousel. I spend more time looking at it instead of looking out for my suitcase. We then gather together with the other competitors and board the chartered bus into town. There's a whole lot of excited chatter about gear and race nutrition, and a possible training run today. I join in several conversations at once with people in the seats around me. It's so wonderful to be meeting everyone at last.

We arrive at our hotel and walk tentatively across the slippery ice towards the safety of the doormat. I don't want to have come all this way just to slip over in the carpark!

News is, that our race briefing will be at 6pm tonight. I unpack my gear and Doug and I have a short walk through town. There's a supermarket, a coffee shop, and a great-looking restaurant in the pub. I post a letter to Santa Claus and we put on our surf lifesaving uniforms for a picture next to the harbour. It's so chilly! The afternoon flies by.

We meet up in the conference room for our briefing. There are forty-four other competitors from twenty-two different countries. All up, including me, there are thirty-five men and ten women, of all ages and race experience. In this mix are six Aussies—Jon Brand, Simon Cariss, Adrian Dodson-Shaw, Marcus Fillinger, Douglas Wilson, and me.

We hear from the race medic, Dennis Andrade, a highly experienced doctor who has worked in these extreme conditions many times before. He talks about managing our body temperature, educates us in recognising and avoiding frost nip and frost bite, and gives us tips on how to cope with the race itself. Dennis informs us he'll be stationed in the heated aid tent to keep an eye on us as the race unfolds. We'll be in good hands.

Richard Donovan, the race organiser, discusses running gear and race nutrition and exactly where the race will take place—it will be 12 laps around the temporary Russian base, called Camp Barneo. It's been set up on a sizeable, stable icefloe up at the North Pole. We'll be sharing the facilities with international adventurers, research scientists and the amazingly resilient Russians.

He explains that there's a graded airstrip to land on and heated tents to sleep and eat in, and that the temperature at the North Pole can drop dramatically, so we need to be prepared. There's 24-hour daylight at this time of year, as the sun never leaves the sky. And one more thing, there could be polar bears … but we'll be supervised and protected by armed personnel.

*Okay …*

Following the race we'll all have the opportunity to fly up in helicopters to stand on the exact coordinates of the Geographic North Pole—in other words, we'll be on the very top of the world. *Wow! This has been something that up until now, I'd only ever dreamed about. But it's true. I'm actually going to be there!*

We're presented with our race packs, which contain our race bibs and T-shirts and neck buffs. I'm number sixteen. My heart is racing as I pull my T-shirt on. Now this race is feeling real. We have our photos taken, firstly as individuals, then as a group. Fittingly we pose in front of another taxidermied polar bear—this one is rearing up in the hotel foyer. It's mighty white frame towers far above us. *I had no idea they were so big.*

Dinner is a serious 'carbohydrate loading' feast at the hotel bar: pasta, pizza or soup with bread. It's great to get to know people.

We have another day until we fly out, so we go dog sledding and explore about town. I buy a new balaclava that fits more snuggly and I head off, fully kitted, to test things out on a training run. I stick close to the roads and stop before the polar bear sign on the far edge of town. My legs are feeling fresh; my trail runners are gripping well in the snow; my goggles are clear and every inch of my skin is covered. *Perfect. This all works for me.*

I return to the room to find Doug's made up a new nick-name for me: The Arctic Shadow. It makes me laugh. I feel so blessed to have Doug here. His support is unbelievable and to share this experience together in the lead-up to the race gives me a whole lot of additional comfort, company and reassurance.

The next day we have our gear for the North Pole packed ready to go, waiting for the announcement to load up the bus. Our bags are going to the airport three hours ahead for weighing and loading onto the plane. The weather is looking good. The word is, 'Go!' So the bus heads off.

We've been broken up into two groups to travel to the North Pole. I'm in group one, on the first plane to fly. The bus returns to the hotel carpark and we climb onboard with our daypacks and bulky polar jackets and boots. We have to squeeze into our seats.

Doug comes on the bus, he's going to take photos and wave me goodbye. He sits next to me, and I lean my head on his shoulder as we drive past the harbour and the little houses. I'm feeling incredibly emotional, wishing he could come too.

We disembark and walk into the cargo terminal. All around us are boxes and crates. It's a rare glimpse into the logistics required to keep this remote Norwegian town of Longyearbyen functioning and fed.

We wait near the roller door that leads out onto the tarmac. Richard checks we're all okay and accompanies the Russian ground staff around as they mark our names off their list. Out there on the tarmac our plane is almost ready to go.

It's an Antonov An-74TK-100 aircraft. A stocky, powerful, purpose-built Russian passenger/cargo plane that has the capability to fly to, and land in, the world's most extreme locations—at altitude, on icefloes in the Arctic and glaciers in the Antarctic. I watch as our bags are loaded one by one via the rear ramp in the fuselage.

Then it's time for a group photo. 'North Pole Marathon!' we all shout to a number of cameras.

I give Doug a hug and walk towards the plane with my red backpack slung over my shoulder. TG is safely tucked away inside.

'Go get 'em, Arctic Shadow!' Doug sings out.

I turn and laugh and give him a wave.

Inside the Antonov, it's a functional, working shell. It's has a half seating, half cargo hold. *Who needs fancy when you're going on an adventure?* I find a seat and rest my backpack and jacket on my knees. I do up my seatbelt low and tight and take a deep breath in.

The Antonov is piloted and crewed by Russians who fly with a whole lot of skill and bravado. They have the intuition and the confidence to handle these extreme elements. You can tell these men never become afraid. They're big and bold

*Running the North Pole Marathon.*
CREDIT: MARK CONLON

*Crossing the finish line of the North Pole Marathon.*
CREDIT: MARK CONLON

*Aussies at the Geographic North Pole: L–R Simon Cariss, Adrian Dodson-Shaw, HH and Rob De Castella.*

PHOTOGRAPHER: HEATHER HAWKINS

*In Paris, and on my way home to Australia after the North Pole Marathon… the race that changed my life!*

CREDIT: DOUG HAWKINS

*Race lap dedications for the 100 kilometre ultra marathon at Centennial Park, August 2015.*
CREDIT: HEATHER HAWKINS

*World Marathon Challenge in Antarctica, pre-race with the flags and medals for each continent.*

CREDIT: SARAH ADLER AMES

*Miami Leg of the World Marathon Challenge (marathon #3) with Alvin Matthews on the finish line.*

CREDIT: RICHARD DONOVAN WMC

*A family hug at the final finish line of the World Marathon Challenge in Sydney.*

CREDIT: GLENN DUFFUS

*Climbing Amphu Labtsa Pass, Great Himalaya Trail.*
CREDIT: TSERING LAMA

*Doing it tough on the trail.*
CREDIT: CALLUM HAWKINS

*Completion of the Great
Himalaya Trail, Tibetan border.
Left to right: Matt Taylor;
Rebekah Hawkins; HH;
Callum Hawkins.*
CREDIT: LAKPA SHERPA

*On the trail with TG the Bear.*
CREDIT: CALLUM HAWKINS

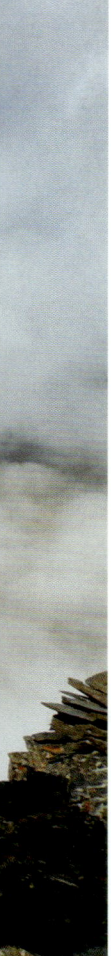

*Trail running with Bek and Matt in October 2016.*
CREDIT: SYDNEY TRAIL SERIES

*New York Marathon 2016 as the Can Too ambassador.*
CREDIT: NYC MARATHON

*With Doug at beautiful Coogee Beach, April 2017.*

CREDIT: DOUGLAS FROST

like polar bears. They welcome you onboard with a nod and there's a whole conversation there, but they don't say a word. The pilots move into the open cockpit while the navigator sits himself down at his gauges and dials. Another crew member distributes earplugs. The forward cabin door is closed.

It's dim in here, except for beams of daylight peeping through the portholes at the front and the rear. In the seat pocket in front of me there's a Russian emergency procedure card. I study it for a moment or two, but give up.

The engines roar. Then like a slingshot, we're thrust in the air. It's the shortest take-off I've ever experienced. The plane banks steeply, climbs steadily and heads north. I take my earplugs out and chat with Marianna Zaikova, who's in the seat next to me. She's just completed the World Marathon Challenge and I'm so inspired. I file that race away for another day.

The in-flight service is a welcome bottle of water and sandwiches. I close my eyes and try to doze. There's still another hour to go.

As the plane prepares to land, we pull on our jackets and get our balaclavas and gloves ready to slip on. It's not the normal preparation for disembarking. There's no tray tables to stow or seats to return to the upright position. No window shades to lift up because, well, there are *no* windows here in the middle of the plane.

*We're about to land!*

We descend … and descend … and then the tyres touch the ice. It's such a different sound to landing on a normal runway. There's scraping and sliding and crunching. It lasts a long time. I hold my breath, praying the plane will stop soon, and not slide clean off the edge, or crack through the ice and plummet into the sea. The engines are roaring. The cargo is shifting forward in the nets.

Then we slow right down. *Hooray!* Relief washes over the entire cabin and we clap. The Antonov turns and taxis back to the base camp, and then its engines are cut.

Everyone's up, putting on beanies, gloves and buffs. The excitement is palpable. *What will it be like out there?* The forward door is opened and a ladder is set in place. We file out one by one.

I've pictured this moment from the day that I registered. That I'd step off the plane and there would be blue sky, polar bears and bright white ice. But when I finally get to the doorway to look out, it's all so white! In fact, everything's white—the sky, the snow, everything. It's the closest thing to a white-out that I can imagine! *These Russian pilots are remarkable!*

As I climb down the ladder the wind whips wildly at my clothes. It's cold! I mean, really, really cold! I laugh at myself, and think, *really, what else was I expecting?* I reach the end of the ladder and take my first few tentative steps out on the graded runway. It's surreal. Like walking on the moon. We all huddle around the plane to get photos.

Curiosity gets the better of me and I scrape at the thin layer of snow. Beneath my boots appears thick, translucent blue ice. There's no land below, simply snap-frozen sea. It's completely mesmerising. This is a wild, temporary place—shifting, drifting, melting, cracking—and this ice that I'm standing on right now, is on limited time, and I can feel it's cold creeping in through my soles.

I take turns taking photos with Annie Rawlinson, then gather up my yellow duffle bag and walk towards camp. Flags with the Camp Barneo logo are flying straight out in the strengthening breeze.

The base is a cluster of large blue tents and generators. On it's perimeter sit fuel drums and helicopters and snowmobiles.

The whole scene before me shouts out 'adventure and daring'. It makes me wonder how those early adventurers survived. Here we are, clad in waterproof everything and goose down, with heated tents and satellite phones, when all they had was wool, leather and fur, and unwavering courage.

I head to tent number four, and I'm sharing this with eight other women. I step up through a raised wooden door with an old metal handle. There are stretcher beds set up, five either side. I choose one in the middle on the left side—it's away from the door. I'm between Annie and Alice, and across the way from Audrey. We unpack a little and chat. The diesel generator hums on and hot air gushes through a large flexible silver duct at the rear. *It's so toasty and lovely in here*—cocooned from the elements and drawing strength from each other.

But it's time for lunch so we wander to the mess tent. As we open the door, the noise hits us—it's filled with international adventurers, scientists, helicopter pilots, Russians, and a whole lot of marathoners. It's an amazing place to be.

Russian chefs bring out large silver pots of rice and pasta, vegetables and goulash from the kitchen tent. I have some rice first, and then make up one of my dehydrated meals from home. I listen to fascinating stories from members of a British expedition. I talk with a gallant helicopter pilot called Captain Q, and get to know some more of my fellow marathoners better. There's Gary Seery and Paul Grealish from Ireland. And from the USA, there's Mark Collins, Karen Curtis, and her partner, York Naylor Schueller, who's here to support her.

Richard updates us with some news—because of the unfavourable flying conditions, the second plane will be delayed until tomorrow. Hopefully things will improve. I have a cup of strong, black Russian tea then venture back to my tent to write in my diary, hug TG the Bear and settle in for some sleep.

As I drift off I picture the sun trekking around the horizon, not over it ... it will have no time to sleep ...

The next day, the weather has cleared and the second plane lands with the remaining competitors. I'm relieved. Now the race can proceed.

We gather for a final briefing in the mess tent. Race start time is announced: 1.30pm. The marathon course is to be a 12-lap course in the soft snow around the airstrip and the base. It will be marked out with little black flags, so we must always remember to keep them on our right. There will be strategically placed support staff with rifles just in case polar bears wander onto the course.

There's a heated aid tent set up with tables for us to place our race nutrition on and this will be manned by our race medic, Dr Dennis Andrade, a Russian military medic and Kate Richardson, a lovely race support person. They will all keep an eye on us. In here we'll be able to defrost our goggles, switch gloves, warm up and refuel.

It's 12.30pm. There's only one hour to go until the race starts.

I gather all my race nutrition together and set up my area on the table where my number sixteen is attached. I lay out my chocolate, my snakes, my gels, my bottled water. I stand back and look at it, then look around the room. I honestly can't believe I'm here!

Steve Hill from Britain is number seventeen. There is a chair for us to share. We exchange words of encouragement: 'All the best for the race'; 'We can do this'; 'I'll look out for you, out there'; 'I promise to share this chair!'

*Not long now* ... I wander back to tent number four.

I lay out my spare socks and extra thermals on my bed. I tie my surf lifesaving cap on over my beanie and balaclava.

I have every inch of skin covered. I clip my race number around my waist. I've got everything I need. I eat chocolate, put my toe warmers into my shoes and my hand warmers into my mitts. I'm ready to go.

I give TG the Bear a hug and sit on my bed for a moment or two. I'm focused and quiet, clear-minded and calm. I read through my list of people that I'm dedicating the laps too. Then I close my eyes, whisper a prayer, and walk to the start line.

It's time to face this race. To gather up every little part of me, and put it all into play. It's time to tap into all the wisdom and strength that I've gained from every single race before this and every single challenge I've overcome, and call them into action. I know this marathon, up here on this shifting icefloe, will be far beyond anything I've ever faced before.

The words 'North Pole Marathon 2015' stand out in great big letters on the start/finish gate. This looks like a stadium. What's been created here in the ice is remarkable. It's official, this icefloe is now hosting an international event. Flags from every competitor's country are flying freely in the breeze.

I seek out one flag in particular—the Australian flag. I find it. It's on my left. It's a beautiful deep-blue cloth gracefully moving in the wind with all those glorious white stars of the Southern Cross. This flag represents so much—my life, my family. It offers hope and encouragement. It represents home. It also reminds me that this is a competition among twenty-two nations. There are six Aussies running today. Although we signed up for this race on our own, we're united. We'll look out for each other. *Aussie Aussie Aussie, Oi Oi Oi!*

Everyone gathers together. There is a real aura of expectation. The weather conditions are perfect—blue sky, mild winds, and a balmy −28°C.

We dance about nervously on the ice, keeping our feet away from the cold for as much as we can. We're ready to go in to battle against the elements. I'm five rows back from the front. I give Adrian Dodson-Shaw a big, emotional hug and wish him all the best. Marcus Fillinger is at the front of the pack with his huskies. They're keen to run. So am I!

I do a mental check that I have everything I need and that my pockets are zipped, my trail runners are secured and my over mitts are on. My ski goggles add a slight blue tint to everything around me. They haven't fogged up yet, which is a great sign. I hope they stay that way.

Rob de Castella is the starter for the race. He's in his blue jacket and black wind shell pants, and he cuts an iconic figure at the start line. To have him here, the true champion that he is, and to see the care and support he's providing Adrian, as well as to all us other runners, is nothing short of inspirational. Rob lifts the starting hooter and points it to the sky.

I hold my breath! All my expectations are riding on this very moment.

It sounds. *Go!*

This is it. The race is on. I'm off and running, out into the unknown ...

We spill forward, cheering and whooping and raising our hands in the air. All that pent-up energy and emotion and anticipation from all those months leading up to this point comes bursting out. This is what we've trained for. *I'm going to see this race through to the end, no matter how tough the conditions get out here today.*

For the first few metres we're all bunched up, running past the aid tent, past the kennels for Marcus' huskies, past the portaloos on the left and our sleeping tents on the right. Our collective shoes crunch loudly on the ice. Then it's up and over an icy ridge on the edge of camp and this sifts us into single file. Ahead the icy expanse is breathtaking. This part of the course is straight and flat and stretches far off to the horizon.

The fastest men lead out at an amazing pace and soon we're spread out like ants on an icy pole. On our left are five small expedition helicopters and several drums of aviation fuel. *How did those fragile-looking craft fly here? Gallant pilots, I guess.*

I press the button on my headset, my music plays. My phone is tucked away in an inside pocket. 'That's Freedom' by John Farnham fills my ears. It's an Aussie classic and a favourite song of mine. *Perfect,* I think to myself, *this is freedom out here.* My spirits soar.

With every step, Camp Barneo slips away from view. We run parallel to the graded airstrip, following the little black 'North Pole Marathon' flags. They flutter in the breeze, marking our trail and breaking the gruelling 42 kilometres up into bite size, achievable pieces. The surface underfoot is soft snow with a crunchy crust, dotted by small icy sections and ridges in the ice.

I settle into a steady pace. I'm about middle of the line, but I wonder where I am sitting in regard to all the other women. I'm having trouble figuring out who's who, because everyone looks the same in their beanies and big, bulky jackets.

John Farnham sings on …

This is lap one. I have eleven to go. *So far so good.* I'm warm, feeling strong and positive. My feet are sinking down into the snow only to ankle height, and it's actually just like the sand at Coogee Beach. I'm in familiar territory. I think about Mum and Dad—this lap is dedicated to them. My heart wells up. I wish they could be here. They would definitely love this place.

The course turns to the right and skirts the end of the runway. This is encouraging, I feel like I'm making progress. There are some Russians on a snowmobile patrolling the area, they're looking out for us, as well as for polar bears.

John Farnham starts another song—'You're the Voice'—I love this song too. This really helps keep me at a good, controlled pace. I pass a couple of people and wave to them.

Then all of a sudden my music fades. It's like there's an incoming call. *Huh? Hello? Who's calling me up here?* There's silence on the line. I press the button on my headset repeatedly … on and off … nothing. *What's going on, where's my music gone? Where's John Farnham? Have my headphones come loose?* I've got to figure this out.

I slow down to a walk, slip off one of my over mitts and unzip my jacket to check my phone. The screen is blank. *What?* Then it dawns on me … the battery has frozen. *No!* Even though it's been next to my ribs, it's still got too cold for it.

'Well this changes things,' I say, mumbling the obvious. The rest of my race will be without music. I've lost one of the best coping techniques that I know. It's a big mental blow and sets me adrift. *How am I going to cope now?* I'm suddenly shifted away from the familiar rhythm and lyrics of songs, to absolute silence and to an overwhelming dread of relying purely on my thoughts and emotions to run the rest of this race. I zip my jacket back up and put my mitts back on. I've got to pick up my pace and press on regardless.

Soon I reach the other side of the runway, the little black flags are still on my right. The snow has churned up over here already. I concentrate on my core and focus on my footing. I try to run tall to stop wobbling around. A gentle breeze blows. I adjust my hood forward.

As this lap unfolds, I reflect further on my parents. Of their love and encouragement. Of how much I miss them. I think back to the Tanami Track and the hot, dusty days in the 4WD. To the cool autumn bushwalks with Mum in the mountains near Warburton. To snippets of our precious conversations. To their wisdom, their faith, their strengths and their frailties. To their hugs. To their determination and sense of adventure and love of life. *They'd love it up here!*

I run on with these thoughts and the disappointment about my music soon melts away. I begin to realise that losing all my songs is perhaps the best thing that could have happened to me. This race is becoming so much more meaningful and profound.

Soon I'm skirting the other end of the runway and heading back towards camp. I look up in either direction and wonder if we'll see a plane come in today. A few metres away there's a small icy section to negotiate, then I'm into the last kilometre of this loop. My pace remains strong, so much so, I'm really warming up and beginning to get thirsty. I take off one mitt and reach into my left outer pocket for my water. But the neck of the plastic bottle's frozen stiff, and so are my glucose gels. *Well, this changes things too.* I'll need to adapt my race plan and make sure I stop at the aid tent every lap. That's really going to slow me down, but on the positive side, at least I'll avoid carrying any extra weight and it will cut down any unnecessary exposure.

Up ahead I see the two Russian MI-8 helicopters. They stand out against the snow with their bright orange and blue colouring. To the right of them are the flags and the graded chute to the finish line. There are lots of runners stretching out in front of me. I remind myself not to be discouraged and that it doesn't matter where I am. I just need to run my own race, and make it all the way through.

I run past another guard on polar bear watch. He's got a rifle slung over his shoulder and binoculars in his hands. This is definitely something you don't see at a city marathon. And I'm glad I'm not wearing white.

Only another 500 metres to go of lap one. I start to plan my stop at the aid tent. I'll unload my water and frozen race gels. Leave my phone. Take off my mid-fleece layer as I'm starting to sweat. I can hear Richard's and Dennis' wise words: 'Manage your core temperature'. I'll try to do this change over as efficiently as I can, as there's still eleven laps to go.

I'm onto the graded ice of the chute. I look longingly at the Aussie flag. I run past Fearghal Murphy, who's tasked with documenting the laps and times of runners. I wave and sing out 'hello!' He waves back and confirms that that's lap one done.

I disappear into the tent and find my race number on the table, and unload. There are so many people in here, adjusting gear, talking animatedly. Dr Dennis and Kate ask me if I'm okay. I reassure them I'm feeling strong. I eat a few squares of chocolate, have a drink, put my mitts on, and balaclava, and head out the door.

Onto lap two.

Up and over the ice ridge, past the expedition helicopters and out along the straight stretch. I feel good. I overtake another runner and reach out to give them an encouraging touch on their shoulder. They give me the thumbs up.

This lap is dedicated to my husband, Doug. I think about how we met, our first date, our wedding, the business, the amazing support he's been over the past twenty-five years of marriage. I wish he was here with me now. I run past the Russians on the snowmobile.

Then my goggles start to fog up at the bottom, and ice crystals form. I'm worried. This is not meant to happen.

*What am I going to do? How long can I keep them on before they completely fog up? If I take them off, I'll expose my eyes. If I wipe them inside I'll damage the anti-fog film.* Panic begins to rise.

Fortunately, the fog stops midway. I can still see through the top. I tilt my head down to compensate. It means my neck stiffens up, but I have no other option. I'll just have to get through these next few kilometres, push through this discomfort and defrost them at the end of this lap.

Along the horizon, the sun is making the snow glow a gentle gold, it's trying it's best to keep us warm. I run around the end of the airstrip and turn. *Crunch, crunch,* the splintering crust is so loud. Across the icy section and past the armed guard. The parked helicopters come back into view and I turn onto the chute and run. That's lap number two. I'm into the tent and defrosting my goggles.

Lap number three, I dedicate to my children, Bek and Cal. I love them so much. I think back to their years growing up, from toddlerhood to their first days at school, to their teenage years and to the adults that they've become. Over the years our roles have gradually shifted from being parent/child, to being close friends. I'm exceptionally proud of them and hope that one day they'll get to have an experience like this too. I have a feeling they will—they both have adventurous spirits. And anything I can do that will encourage them to explore and travel and push their boundaries even further will make me a truly happy mum.

As I round the corner at the end of the runway, I notice a crack in the ice. I'm sure it wasn't there before. I must let Richard and Fearghal know. The snow is so chopped up in this middle section. Some runners have slowed to a walk. I give Annie Rawlinson a hug and encourage her along.

Back onto the chute, that's another lap done.

Lap four I run for ovarian cancer sufferers. I look down at the little teal ribbon flapping on the collar of my jacket. It signifies so much. It's been eight years since I started my journey. I feel so fortunate to be out here, running like this, and hope it will bring some strength to those who need it to fight their way through and encouragement to come out the other side, even stronger.

I think about all those incredibly brave women that I met along the way: in the waiting rooms, in the hospital corridors and lifts, recovering from surgery, undergoing chemotherapy, waiting for results, losing their battle against this horrible disease. I'm running for them today and praying that they can all pull through.

On lap five, I start to see the effects of the extreme cold. The toe warmers in my shoes are freezing into little ice blocks beneath my feet. They're uncomfortable and cold. I guess they're not working. I've got to get them out.

Instead of stopping off at the aid tent, I race straight for tent number four and sit on my camp bed. In here my friend, Alice Burch from Great Britain, is changing her wet socks. We chat and then she's off. She's running so well.

I fumble about with my laces and shoes. I know time is of the essence, but my fingers aren't working well. I peel away my thick outer socks and take out the toe warmers. They're little solid rocks! I leave them on the floor. My inner socks feel damp, so I change these too, and wriggle my runners back on. I backtrack to the aid tent to grab some chocolate and check in with Dr Dennis and Kate. Then I'm back on the course for lap number six, over the ridge and onto the straight.

The sun treks around further. I keep an eye on the crack in the ice and jump over it. Still no signs of polar bears.

I wonder what the time is, and how long each lap is actually taking me. I can only guess, as I can't get to my watch beneath all these layers.

Lap number six is for friends. From childhood, and church, from high school and nursing, my neighbours and friends from our work. There's one friend in particular who comes to my mind, Eric Mallard. He has been a friend of mine since the 1970s. I was twelve when he had his accident; he was just a teenager. He was swimming in the Yarra River and dived in and hit his head. He suffered extensive spinal damage, and would have drowned in the fast-flowing water was it not for the bravery of his friends.

There were tough early days for Eric in hospital and rehabilitation, but it was his courageous spirit, determination and faith that got him through. And he never gave up. He adjusted to life in a wheelchair, learned to drive, studied, became a lecturer and continues to push through to this day. I've drawn so much strength and inspiration from him, over all these years.

Now it's my turn to give back. I'll run for him. I'll be his legs today, and so I pick up my pace and cry. I pass more people out around the runway. This is the halfway mark. *We're nearly there! Nearly … ha … not!*

Lap seven I run for Matthew Hall, the son of an Englishman, Chris Hall, who we'd met on the plane to Paris. Matthew had tragically passed away at a young age, six years before. As any parent who had been through something like this, the loss was still there today, so I promised I would run a lap in memory of Matthew. Because seven had been Matthew's favourite number, this is the lap for him. It's a fast lap, a good lap, and my heart carries me along.

During lap eight, the conditions begin to change. The wind picks up. The snow sweeps in on strengthening gusts. I'm protected when it's blowing from behind, as my hood shelters me well, but then as I turn the runway corner it finds a gap between my balaclava and goggles and chills one side of my face. I move my neck buff up to try to stop the gap. It freezes into position. It's stiff like cardboard.

The sky is white, and the sun has gone. It's bleak, extreme and challenging. The temperature plummets to −41°C. It would be perfectly understandable to become overwhelmed, dismayed, beaten. But I steel myself and tell myself that if there's no comfort to be found outside, then I'll need to find it inside. So I gather all the positive thoughts I can and keep them running on a continuous loop through my head.

*I'm already two thirds of the way through. I'm running steadily. There's chocolate to look forward to in the aid tent. My thermal underwear was a brilliant investment.* It all helps to keep a smile on my face and as surprisingly simple as it may seem, this positivity actually keeps me going strong.

The track is a little more compressed in parts, but other sections are completely chopped up. Up and down over small ridges. Now the wind is blasting my front. I lean into it and run. My wind shell pants are blown against the thermals on my thighs. I can feel the cold, but I try to ignore it. *No distractions. I'm fine.* My footprints are quickly covered by a new layer of snow. The little black flags are beacons of hope. Like friends showing the way, flapping, clapping, willing me on.

Past the parked helicopters, along the firm, icy chute, past Richard and Fearghal, who count off this lap, I head into the medic tent to have the much-anticipated chocolate and water. Steve Hill is in here, as well as Adrian Dodson-Shaw. They're courageously pushing along.

But there's several other competitors starting to show signs of exhaustion and the beginnings of hypothermia. The vigilant medics retire them from the race and remind us all to keep every piece of skin covered. My surf lifesaving cap is tied over my beanie and it's keeping my balaclava anchored in place, and teamed up with my goggles and hood, everything's pretty much intact right now.

Lap nine—I run on. I'm currently third place female. I pass Jennifer Cheung and move into second place.

At the end of the tenth lap I have a quick stop in the tent to grab a drink. Alice is there, adjusting her goggles. It dawns on me that she must be in first place. I've actually caught up with her. And so I make a bold move. Instead of stopping to rest and defrosting my balaclava, I grab a couple of jelly snakes and made a break for it and move into the lead.

I run lap eleven like I've never run before. I try to put as much distance between Alice and myself as possible. I don't look back. Up over the snow ridges, stumbling in places but managing to stay upright. Following the little black flags.

*Run, run, I've got to stay in front! I can't lose this position now. This is my one chance. I can't let it slip away. I've got to be determined and strong. Run, run, forwards, on and on. Eyes down, eyes forward.*

My hood blocks my peripheral vision. I can't see where anyone is. I run on. My hands are cold. I roll them into balls and my large mitts hang down like limp broken limbs. Over the icy section, I turn the corner around the runway, past the helicopters and into the chute. There's the Aussie flag with all its stars and blue sky. One more lap to go.

Lap twelve—my final lap. Richard confirms I'm in the lead as I pass the start/finish gate. I run into the aid tent, grab two jelly snakes and a mouthful of water and burst out the door. There's no looking back. There's fire in my heart. I don't feel the cold anymore and the snow doesn't seem quite as deep. I'm running just like the wind that's whipping against my frame.

I think of my mum and dad, Doug, Bek and Cal.

Round the first corner of the runway, over the slushy crack and into the deeper snow.

I call out to Eric, my friend, and tell him that I'm running as fast as I can for him. I'm his legs!

I think about my brothers, my extended family and friends, of Matthew and his dad … I run on and on.

The wind is wild and visibility is low. I put my head down and I run and run. This race is for all those with ovarian cancer.

Onwards, faster, I have to stay in the lead. I run another long corner, over the ice patch, around the other end of the runway, and finally closer to the helicopters. I can see the flags flying. The Australian flag is there. I swallow the snakes that I've held in my cheek for this entire lap.

I'm nearly there … just 500 metres to go. I try to think of something to say at the finish line. I run … and run … onto the firm ice, along the chute, and I stride out as fast as I possibly can.

They're stretching the ribbon across the finish. They're standing with cameras on the other side. I've never done this before. Never been the *winner* in a marathon. The Aussie flag is on the left. I've passed it eleven times, and now I can reach for it and lift it high!

*It's time. I'm here. My race is run!*

Tears, elation and sheer relief wash over me. The ribbon curls its way around my waist and the flag flies valiantly out. I raise my arms. It's only taken me 6 hours, 57 minutes and 39 seconds to get here and create one of the most memorable moments of my life!

I pull my balaclava down. Everything is frozen. My hood, my neck buff, even some of my hair. I talk in bursts, brimming with emotion.

'That was unreal.'

'What a special race.'

'Thank you, Richard!'

Richard places the race medal around my neck. He gives me a hug and says, 'Well done to you, Heather!'

Mark Conlon, the official race photographer, snaps a close-up pic and captures this moment in time. Even today, as I look at this image, tears well up. I can see the joy, the exhaustion, the personal triumph of that day. I see the change in me, and the hint of growing courage within, and the realisation that with willpower anything is possible. And that this signifies another new beginning in my running journey, one which will take me from this finish line into a whole new world of extremes.

There are flecks of ice building on my exposed cheeks. My freckles are there on my face and my flattened curls peep out from beneath my beanie. It's evidence that it's me under there. In my ski goggles are the reflections of those who made this adventure happen—Richard Donovan, the amazing race organiser, and those who recorded the adventure—Dave Painter and Mark Conlon. I can't thank them enough.

I walk off to the race tent. I'm quiet, but on the inside my heart is singing. I open the wooden door and Petr Vabrousek, the champion triathlete and male winner of the marathon, is first to hug and congratulate me. He asks, 'Would you like a hot cup of tea?'

'Yes, please, that would be awesome!' I reply.

I'm shaking all over but I'm okay. It's joy, it's exhaustion, it's relief, it's not the cold.

I can't wait to share the news with my family and I imagine Doug saying, 'Hey! Well done to you, Arctic Shadow!'

I fumble with the ties on my surf lifesaving cap, as they're stuck in a frozen knot beneath my chin. My iced-up balaclava and buff are wedged firmly underneath. The Russian medic sees my predicament and comes over with his bear-like hands and deftly unties the knot. He speaks to me in Russian in the deepest rumble I have ever heard, but it's with a gentleness that defies his towering frame. He hands me my cap and gives me a nod and hugs me in his huge polar bear arms.

I peel off the icy outer layers and hang them over a chair near the hot air vent. I fold up my race number and put it in my pocket. As I sip my hot cup of tea I look around—the tent is filled with activity and chatter.

Other runners are struggling with exhaustion and cold. I help to warm them up and get them food and help them on their way. There's no urgency to tell anyone I've won, I quietly get on with things. They're doing it tough. I'm not.

I console others who are physically unable to finish the race. I'm devastated for them. There are no words to help their heartache. I simply sit with them, hold them and cry.

I celebrate with Alice and Jennifer, second and third place women. I hug Audrey, who is the fourth woman home. I congratulate Michael Baer and Arthur Kadar on their fabulous runs.

Finally, it's time for some food. I have a bowl of rice and goulash, straight from two large pots in the kitchen tent. Then I race out to the finish line. News is that Adrian's coming in! I'm so excited and happy for him. It's been an epic race. I chat excitedly with Rob de Castella. We clap wildly as Adrian crosses the finish line. *What a moment! The first Indigenous Australian to visit the North Pole and the first to run a marathon here!*

I pack up my leftover gels and drinks and go back to tent number four. I sit on my camp bed and gaze at my medal. I'm amazed. I still can't believe that I've won. To think that for all those years, ever since primary school, my running legs have remained idle, hidden away, curled up in bed as I've recovered from surgery, and now they've managed to carry me through the toughest conditions I've ever experienced in life and kept up with my determined spirit inside.

I'm absolutely elated. And somehow I've beaten the odds.

I've survived cancer. I've turned fifty. I'm an Aussie surf lifesaver from the beach. I'm a mum, a wife, a sister, a daughter, just a regular suburban lady who'd simply found her old runners and gardening shorts in the back of the wardrobe three years ago and got out there and run.

Then suddenly it's midnight, the middle of the night, but it looks more like the middle of the day. The wind's blowing wildly and fresh flecks of snow chase each other across the icefloe. We're standing outside the door of the Camp Barneo mess tent with our bulky jackets and warm boots on, chatting about the race and waiting to board the MI-8 helicopters that'll fly us up to the Geographic North Pole. I'm incredibly tired—running on pure joy and adrenaline right now.

We walk in a group past the finish line. Fearghal and Richard are still there keeping an eye on a couple of remaining competitors out on the course. They're due to finish soon. The flags remain lined up, flapping fervently.

We fill the two helicopters and take off. The massive rotors stir up the snow. Soon we're flying low and fast above the pack ice. Below us are ridges and cracks, and glimpses of ocean. It seems so much colder, and wilder up here. Forty minutes later the navigator signals to the pilot to land. We touch down. We're here: the Geographic North Pole! I climb out. I have my surf lifesaving uniform on over my gear and TG the Bear in my arms. I raise the red and yellow surf lifesaving flag and let it fly. This is freedom out here. My spirits soar … again!

It's the 12 April 2015. I remember it so well.

My races for 2015 don't end there, as I keep on running.

The Centennial Park Ultra is the next one on my list, all 100 kilometres of it. I've had this race in my sights for a little while now. I'm aware it's going to be extremely tough. This is a distance way beyond any I've ever run before, and without a doubt it will test my skills and strength to their absolute limits. But it will be a landmark race, and take me another step forward, perhaps even a leap forward, in my running journey to date.

But in my training runs prior to the day, due to time constraints, I only manage to get to 67 kilometres in one go. All the kilometres beyond that point in the race will carry me into unknown territory. It's also a daunting thought to think I'll be facing 28.5 laps on the dirt track at Centennial Park, with a strict time limit of 12 hours to complete the course.

The night before I write up a list of all the people I'll dedicate the laps to on my left arm in permanent marker. This way I'll be able to refer to them as I go. I fill an esky with cool drinks, chips, gels, chocolate, and bananas, and stick a big 'H' on the lid so it will be easy to find.

I'm going to have to be self-sufficient, because Doug and Cal are overseas training surf lifesavers in Israel, and Bek and her boyfriend, Matt, are working until 4pm. They'll drive over as soon as they can for my final few laps.

The race starts at 6am, in the dark, with our head torches on. As I finish the first lap, the sky's lightening in the east and then by lap three and four there's blue sky and sunshine, and the temperature's quickly on its way to 26°C.

I start off well. Keeping a steady, comfortable 5.5–6 minute kilometre pace. I stop every second lap for a brief sit down on the 'H' on my esky, and to have some food. All is going well until lap sixteen, when my core begins to heat up badly.

Another runner, Katie Lack, who's completing the 50-kilometre race, is a godsend. She sources bags of ice for me to put down my top while I run. It cools me down and I can't thank her enough for this. Another friend, Warren Williams, helps out on the aid station and his encouraging words and smile lift my spirits every time I see him.

One by one I count the laps down. It's a long afternoon. Normal people are on their rugs having picnics in the park, and I watch several soccer matches start and end. Bek and Matt arrive and take turns running in the horse lane on the other side of the white fence to me. Then the sun slips behind the fig trees and the park begins to empty.

Time is getting away from me … I need to pick up my pace … I still have two more laps to go. We put our head torches back on. Warren, Bek and Matt run with me. Now there's only one lap to go. I'll have to do this fast to make it before the cut-off time. It's completely dark. I'm only one of two competitors remaining on the course.

My support crew hangs in there with me. When I reach the aid station at the halfway mark for the very last time, a guy who's been there all day, runs with me too. The support of these four amazing people is what gets me through. Somehow my legs keep going … somehow I manage to stay upright … there are shadows and dips and tree roots to negotiate …

I can't see the names written on my arm anymore, but they're in my heart and I know they've run with me today. The lights of the finish line appear. I cross it with less than 7 minutes to spare, having just run my fastest lap of the day!

The race director, Keith Hong, gives me a big hug and presents me with my finisher's medal and a trophy for third place female. *Wow!* Now that was a complete surprise. Eleven hours, 53 minutes of pure, punishing, personal challenge.

Twelve hours later I hobble onto a plane to join Doug and Cal to teach surf lifesaving in Israel. I disembark in Tel Aviv and literarily hit the ground running, soon feeling the sand of Beersheva Beach, Ashdod, in between my toes. It's the height of summer, absolutely baking, and we run early morning training sessions for adults in the 26°C waters of the Mediterranean, and also help to establish the children's Nipper program here.

I finish the year off with the Blackmores Sydney Full Marathon, back to the location of my very first marathon.

And all through this, I begin to think about what I could do next, how I could push myself further … and I remember an event that I'd filed away for a later date. So I investigate it further and sign up for the World Marathon Challenge.

# Chapter Ten

# THE WORLD MARATHON CHALLENGE

## *The Race of a Lifetime*

## 2016

On my bedside table sits a small, colourful diary. Its cover is an attractive montage of old-fashioned postcards, butterflies, bluebirds, and my favourite flowers, ranuculus.

But, don't let these meek and mild images mislead you, for on the inside there are many bold and spirited words about a daring dream. So much has spilled onto these pages—ideas, determination, heartbreak, hope and tears—and maybe even a drop of perspiration or two.

For this precious little diary holds my journey of the 2016 World Marathon Challenge (WMC). I remember my preparation for this race vividly …

The first entry in my diary, along its faint blue lines, is a race dedication plan. I keep up my little personal tradition to make every run into a run for others. It gives me an additional purpose, propels me through all those kilometres, because I know I'm not running it alone.

**1 October 2015**
**Race Dedications for the World Marathon Challenge**

> *Dedicating the overall race to Mum and Dad – continuing on*
> *   their legacy*
> *Dedicating individual marathons to:*
> *Union Glacier – Mum and Dad, surf lifesaving friends*
> *Punta Arenas – Doug, Bek and Cal*
> *Miami  – Trevor, Ray and extended family*
> *Madrid – all my friends in life*
> *Marrakesh – to the future, to life and faith*
> *Dubai – all those affected by ovarian cancer*
> *Sydney – the Can Too Foundation, Surf Lifesaving Australia,*
> *   Aussies and celebrating life!*

On the next page I jot down some inspiring words:

> *'If I ride the wings of the morning,*
> *If I dwell by the farthest oceans,*
> *even there Your hand will guide me*
> *and Your strength will support me …'*

I scrawl a funny throwaway line diagonally across the page:
   'Seven is my favourite number and running in circles is my thing.'

I itemise my song playlist and it's brimming with great Aussie classics, such as:

*'Great Southern Land' – by Icehouse*
*'One Country' – by Midnight Oil*
*'Under the Milky Way Tonight' – by The Church*

On the next page I make a list of all the gear I need:

✓ *Compression socks and recovery compression tights for the plane*
✓ *6 pairs of running shorts and singlets*
✓ *Trail runners from the North Pole Marathon*
✓ *2 pairs of road runners*
✓ *Warm gear for Antarctica*
✓ *Hydration backpack*
✓ *Teal ovarian cancer ribbon*
✓ *Surf lifesaving cap*
✓ *Can Too foundation singlet*
✓ *TG the Bear*
✓ *Race gels and nutrition*
✓ *2 tracksuits*
✓ *Sunscreen and lip balm*
✓ *Chocolate, potato chips, dehydrated meals*
✓ *Skin lubricant spray and medical kit*
✓ *Passport*
✓ *US dollars*

Once I finish these lists, it's time for me to start planning my specific training for the World Marathon Challenge. I need to take my current running fitness and ramp it up to a whole new level. I know it's going to be gruelling, time-consuming, even mind-numbingly repetitive, as I run laps to get the kilometres into my legs. But if I stick with it and stay disciplined, it will give me the best chance possible of actually pulling this challenge off. That's 295.36 kilometres in under 168 hours, around the world.

Plus, if I can raise funds for cancer research via my fundraising page for the Can Too Foundation, and encourage others to give things a go, this will make this whole experience an even more wonderful one.

I look at my calendar and choose a date: Tomorrow.

So my next diary entry reads:

*On the 2 of October 2015, my training officially begins!*
*I will run 14 kilometres each day for seven days.*

I write the days of the week down one page and draw a box next to them so I can tick them off and record the actual kilometres run.

Most days I head to Centennial Park early in the morning and do the 3.6-kilometre laps under the green leafy fig trees. Again, I can't help but think this is exactly where it all started back in March 2012. Here, with Bek and Cal, I was preparing for the 4-kilometre Mother's Day Classic fun run. I'm still the same old me, just a little braver perhaps and no longer getting out in my old gardening clothes and runners. I actually have running gear that fits.

To mix up my runs, I add in some hills, and set off along the coastal run from Coogee to Bondi and back. There's stairs on the boardwalk near the cemetery and a steep hill back up to Gordons Bay. I gasp for air as I run, but the wind and the waves spur me on.

With three months to go until the World Marathon Challenge, I run 102 kilometres in one week, and I feel great.

On the 19 October 2015, I take it up a notch. I run 21 kilometres each day for seven days. This means a few more laps each time at Centennial Park, an extra run south on the coastal run and two mornings out seeing the early rays of sun glow on the Opera House tiles. I stride out and run across the Sydney Harbour Bridge. That week I clock up 150.9 kilometres. I'm so excited as I prove to myself that I can at least run half the distance of the World Marathon Challenge.

On the 31 October 2015, I push closer towards my goal. I run 32 kilometres each day for seven days. The weather's getting hotter and by adding an extra 11 kilometres every day, it makes these seven days of training a whole lot tougher.

For five mornings out of the seven, my alarm goes off at 5.30am, and I'm out the door as the paper deliveryman and the rubbish trucks come creeping along my street. I weave past the local shops where the world is waking up, and the delivery vans double park outside the cafés. When I run back, three hours later, the vans are gone, and the coffee machines are in glorious, full swing.

The other two days, I mix it up with two late afternoon runs to see what it's like running on tired legs. It's tough, and the sun races me to the finish line both times. But I do it and tick it off my list. I'm relieved. *I think I can actually do this!*

Right now, it's so hard to concentrate on anything else. If it weren't for Doug taking care of the cooking and food shopping, and meeting me at the park to cheer me on, I don't know how I would survive. I manage to pop back into the real world every now and again, when I'm not in my runners, to do some practical things like feed the pets, wash clothes, bake banana bread, get the car serviced and pay some bills.

On my final run this week, I wear my teal ribbon. It's for encouragement. I want to remind myself of where I've been. I could never have dreamed of doing this, eight whole years ago when I lay in my hospital bed. Back then all I longed for was for life to carry me forward with my family and to never let me go.

I add up all my kilometres and it's a total of 225.8 this week. That's the same distance as running from Sydney to Ulladulla on the South Coast!

On the 14 November 2015, my training schedule kicks into final gear. I plan to do a marathon a week, with shorter runs and recovery swims in between. As I run across the Sydney Harbour Bridge, I look up at the spans and the thousands of pounded rivets and out beyond them to the bright blue sky. Beneath my feet the harbour seems quiet and reflective.

I stop for a breather at the entrance to Luna Park and look at the face at the entrance—in my tired state I tell myself it has big white teeth like me. I arrive at Centennial Park and it's filled with picnickers and people doing completely normal, leisurely, lovely things. I gaze at them longingly and wish I could curl up on their picnic rugs and share their biscuits and cheese … but I pull myself together and I slog it out for a couple more laps.

I have a job to do today, and I remind myself there is purpose to all this madness! I am raising funds and awareness about cancer research to help others. Every single kilometre today is providing me with a stepping stone, taking me further away from being defined by cancer. And all this training is my one-way ticket to being a healthier, more adventurous and motivated me, and I don't intend on catching that return flight back to where I was. I run 42.4 kilometres today.

I buy some knee-high compression socks to trial these on

my next run. They feel firm and I wonder what they'll be like to run in. On my way home I look at the pack and question why I bought pink. I know it's a pretty colour, but what if I'll look like a big fifty-year-old kid?

My 6-kilometre run the next afternoon goes well and they provide great calf support. Better still, no one gives me strange looks. *Fabulous, these will work.*

On the 18 November 2015, I head out the door early and run past the fountains and duck ponds of the Botanical Gardens and across the Sydney Harbour Bridge. I stop for a minute in the middle of the Cahill Expressway to watch the ferries come and go at Circular Quay. The sun is sparkling on the harbour water. Wispy clouds streak the sky. I'm feeling good. I run 42.6 kilometres today.

I increase my core exercises with extra sit-ups, push-ups and planks. This will strengthen my abs and help keep a good running posture. I add a few extra songs to my playlist: 'Dancing on The Ceiling' by Lionel Richie—perfect for Miami; 'Dumb Things' by Paul Kelly—a message to myself for signing up to do a crazy adventure like this.

On the 23 November 2015, I'm sweating up the steps of the Sydney Opera House, past the Art Gallery and running back to Coogee to meet Doug for a swim and coffee at the beach. A whole morning goes just like that. I run 42.3 kilometres today.

Now it's only two months to go until the World Marathon Challenge. My legs are holding up well. No injuries. I'm eating as much as my twenty-year-old son and sleeping more than eight hours a night. I'm weary, which is understandable, but I'm also excited and optimistic.

On the 5 December 2015, I decide to challenge myself with 14 kilometres of hills along the coastal run, then run through the Botanical Gardens and home again. I give today's run a name: from the sea to the city to the sofa! It's a very hot day and when I get back home, I have a long afternoon sleep. I run 42.1 kilometres today.

Four marathons down, three to go!

The next morning, the 6 December 2015, my world comes crashing down. I wake up with a sore, raspy throat. I struggle out of bed and I start to panic. *I don't have time to be sick. Hopefully with a good night's sleep and short, easier runs and swims in the ocean over the coming few days, I'll feel better.*

But unfortunately this is not the case. Over the next few days a cough develops—a soul-destroying, chesty, persistent cough.

I talk things over with my doctor and she starts me on a course of antibiotics. I'm too sick to run, so my training is on hold and I'm gutted. Things have been going so well up until now. I will myself to stay positive. I think of how far I've come, that I'm the fittest I've ever been and that a few days off from training won't have a significant impact. *I'll be back running soon.*

I rest up and listen to my running music, and sleep as much as I possibly can. I tell myself to remain calm and to hold onto hope that things will get better. There's only five weeks to go.

A week later I have to let go of my plan to run three more marathons, instead it's replaced with a regime of panadol, ventolin, throat lozenges and loads of sleep. I'm seriously weakened. I can't even hold a conversation without coughing out the punctuation marks, and I'm breathless walking five blocks to the beach and back.

My confidence is taking an absolute battering. *Can I really pull out of this?*

Doug worries too.

One question keeps burrowing deep into my head—*should I postpone the World Marathon Challenge until 2017?* I wrestle with this devastating dilemma for days. But every time I come close to giving it all away, something inside tells me to hang in there, to rely on my past history, to believe that just like other times in my life I'll bounce back from here.

So I hold off postponing the event and keep alive the hope of competing.

On the 22 December 2015, I pull on my runners and go for a 3-kilometre walk and run. I head to Coogee Headland and stand on my favourite sandstone rock to gaze out at the ocean. I watch as the waves crash over Wedding Cake Island. I think to myself, *I still have time. I can do this. I can get back. It's not impossible.*

I walk home up the hills.

Over the next few days my cough eases to a dry hack. My breathing becomes better.

The next page in my diary specifically reads:

*On the road to recovery.*
  *27 December – 12 kilometres*
*Ran and walked today. Hot, tired, sat on a park bench in Hyde Park feeling defeated, tired and broken. How on earth can I do the World Marathon Challenge when I can't even run 6 kilometres right now? It's my slowest pace ever. I have to recover. I have to stay positive.*
  *28 December – 5 kilometres*
  *29 December – 10 kilometres*
  *30 December – 20.5 kilometres*
*Long slow run, but I did it!*
  *31 December – 5 kilometres*
  *2 January – 22.1 kilometres*

*Okay, maybe I can do the WMC after all!*

*4 January – 5 kilometres*

*5 January – 5 kilometres*

*8 January – 3 kilometres*

*9 January – 7 kilometres*

*Ran in the middle of the day, 27 °C under the shady fig trees at Centennial Park. My average pace is 5 minutes, 16 seconds per kilometre.*

*I bought a takeaway coffee and wandered into the rose garden near the duck ponds to my favourite wooden park bench. Thought about life, people, running (of course!) and …*

✓ *It's about making every day count*

✓ *Making every thought positive*

✓ *Never giving up*

✓ *Ensuring every breath is appreciated*

✓ *That every plan is a different one, a new one, a challenging one that will take me on from here. I am going to do the 2016 World Marathon Challenge!*

On the 17 January 2016, I slide my suitcase off the shelf in our wardrobe and I pack. I need as much gear for this one week as I would need for a whole month away. I fill it to the brim and wrestle to do the zip up.

My red backpack, which I'll be taking as carry-on baggage, contains all my running gear just in case my suitcase is lost. I weigh it on the bathroom scales. It's a whole lot more than the regulation seven kilograms! *What am I going to do?* Then I have a brainwave and transfer things into the pockets of my jacket. I'll carry this over my arm.

I phone my brothers and we plan their flights from Melbourne and Alice Springs, to get them to the finish line in Sydney. It's going to mean so much to have them here. If only Mum and Dad could be here too. I'd give anything for them to share this moment with me, to show them that I am continuing their legacy. That I am an adventurous spirit and it's what they've inspired me to become.

Now there's only one more thing to do—paint an airport sign for the departure gate that says, 'That way and keep going around', and another that says, 'Unreal', my favourite word from the North Pole Marathon.

It's finally the 18 January 2016, and I'm up before the sun because it's impossible to sleep. I've been picturing this day for so long. I may not be in perfect shape, and my training hasn't quite gone to plan, but I'm ready to give this run my all.

At check-in, all goes smoothly. My bags tip the scales at the upper limit, but I'm through. A quick photo in front of the departure sign, then it's time to go.

*It's time to go! This is it. I can't believe it. After all those months of anticipation and preparation, everything is now squeezed into this one little dot of a moment. It's time for me to start this next adventure.*

I squeeze Doug and Cal so tightly and tell them that I love them. It's very hard to let them go. Bek is away overseas, but will be back in time for the final marathon in Sydney.

I hoist my backpack on my shoulder, throw my jacket over my arm and walk towards the departure gate. I turn for one last wave, and then I take my first few steps on this journey—alone. *It's all up to me now.* And just like I waved Doug goodbye in Svalbard, and boarded the plane for the North Pole, I do it again. I'll be the 'Arctic Shadow'. I'll be self-reliant, emotionally steady, and comfortable with going it alone.

But as the plane taxis along the runway, my emotions rise up and I battle to keep the tears inside. I look out the window so no one can see my face. Then I'm off into the sky.

A few hours into the flight I take my diary to write:

### 18 January 2016 – World Marathon Challenge
### 2.23pm

*I'm on my way! It's 14.23 and I'm flying across the Pacific
Ocean to Chile. I'm very emotional. My anticipation levels are
going through the roof. What lies ahead?*

*This challenge is epic. Yet when I rationalise it and break it
down, it's only seven marathons with rests in between. Soon I'll
be home again.*

*I am incredibly thankful for the love and support from
everyone. And for all those people who have made donations to
my fundraising page for Can Too. I can't thank them enough.
The money raised will help to save lives.*

*It's a little scary to be putting myself out there publicly. I'm not
used to this. I really don't want to fail. But I'll give it my best
shot and fly the colours for Can Too, Ovarian Cancer, SLSA and
Aussie mums. It's about staying positive, celebrating life, being
fifty, surviving cancer and being part of an incredible family.*

*Here's the understatement for today: this journey, and the
journey of life, is a very, very big one!*

I stretch my legs frequently and walk around the plane.
It's a long flight and I doze and dream and chat to the Aussie
expat sitting next to me. He gives me some tips on places to
eat and what to see in Punta Arenas—if only I had more time.

As we come in for landing, the peaks of the Andes peep
over the wing. *Hello Santiago.* The first leg of my journey is
complete.

I lug my suitcase off the baggage carousel and join the long
zigzagging line leading to customs. Not too far behind me, I
spot Becca Pizzi, another WMC competitor, from the USA.

Our paths eventually cross and we hug exuberantly over the lane divider. There's so much to talk about, but the queue moves us on and we're taken in opposite directions.

I clear customs and find my way to the domestic terminal to catch my connecting flight to Punta Arenas. As I approach the check-in counter there's a sign reminding passengers of the checked-in luggage allowance: 23 kilograms.

Of course, this is a domestic flight. *Eeek!* I'm well over the weight limit. While the queue snakes along, I transfer as many race gels as I can from my suitcase into my jacket pockets and struggle to zip them up. By the time I reach the front of the queue, my jacket weighs a ton and I'm a puddle of stress and sweat. I step forward and present my passport. They weigh my suitcase—it's a kilogram over weight. I hold my breath … I can't afford to leave anything behind … but they print my boarding pass and wave me through. *What a relief! Things have got to get easier from here as I use up my stash of race nutrition.*

As I sit in the lounge and wait for the boarding call, I wonder if there is anyone else on this flight who's doing the WMC? I don't recognise anyone and I think Becca Pizzi is on a later flight.

However, by the time I arrive in Punta Arenas, I've met Stefan Aumann from Germany and Yusuke Mamada from Japan. The three of us catch a cab to the team hotel and meet Richard Donovan, the race organiser (who was also the organiser of the North Pole Marathon). We then go straight into our race briefing in the conference room.

I recognise and hug Sarah Adler Ames from the USA/ Germany, who'd met me for lunch in Sydney back in July. I also hug Fearghal Murphy who's assisting with race logistics and Dave Painter, the video cameraman, they are two familiar faces from the North Pole Marathon. Dave will be documenting this marathon journey too.

*Well, here we are. It's very surreal.* There will be fifteen of us along with the eight ultra marathon runners who will be running the Antarctic 100-kilometre race.

Richard goes through the race program and the safety instructions, and answers lots of questions. My heart is racing. *This is sensational!* He also announces that Stefan Aumann will be donating funds to the chosen charities of three competitors who clearly demonstrate the spirit of sportsmanship. This is an incredibly generous gesture.

We receive our race packs containing our T-shirts, neck buffs and race numbers—I'm number eight. I peer inside my bag and see there are seven race bibs—one for each continent! *Why am I surprised? I shouldn't be!*

Tomorrow we'll pick up our hire gear for Antarctica and receive a more detailed briefing about the Union Glacier, from the Antarctic Logistics and Expeditions Company.

It's 11pm already and I sit up in bed with a pile of pillows behind me. I quickly check Facebook and emails. There's one really lovely message from the Mayor of Randwick, Counsellor Noel D'Souza. He wishes me well and advises he's made a donation to my Can Too fundraising page. I'm incredibly grateful.

At 11.30pm, I pull up my covers, hug TG the Bear and drift off to sleep.

## Tuesday, 19 January 2016

*I wake early and pull the curtains open. It's such a beautiful soft sunrise over the rooftops of Punta Arenas. Streetlights are switching off, and beyond the statues and the paved promenade are the mighty waters of the Strait of Magellan. After breakfast, I go for a short walk to breathe in the fresh sea air.*

*So much is about to happen … I know these next few days will bring with them so many new experiences. But I'm not frightened. I'm ready to cope with the challenges in the way that I've learned to before—by being practical and never, ever giving up.*

In the foyer they're setting up the scales to weigh our bags for Antarctica. I head upstairs and pull my yellow duffle bag out from my suitcase. It's a matter of packing what I need just for the next few days: clothes to wear around Union Glacier base camp, my race gear and the nutrition for this marathon.

I pack as methodically as I can, then lug the bag downstairs and onto the scales. It only weighs nine kilograms. *Fabulous!* That was easy and I'm not a stressed, sweaty puddle. I load it into the back of a truck to be taken to the airport. Things are looking promising for the plane to fly out either later today or tomorrow morning.

I chat with Patrick Fallon, from the USA, and we have a short 5-kilometre run along the promenade together to shake out the stiffness from our legs. His motivation for doing the WMC is to raise funds for children cancer research in memory of Jonny Wade, a little boy who sadly passed away a few weeks ago from a brain tumour. Jonny's parents will be there in Miami for marathon number three. I look forward to meeting them and giving them a hug.

We all share an impromptu lunch together, and I tuck into a mountainous mushroom risotto. Sarah, Stefan, Becca and I try on our polar clothing. The gear is incredibly warm and we absolutely cook in the change rooms.

Later we're back for our in-depth Antarctic briefing and we're presented with our boarding passes for our flight. I study mine closely. Destination Antarctica! We're one step closer.

This icy location will be the start of our epic marathon journey and I can't wait to get there. My thoughts race with anticipation.

Not long after we return to our hotel, there's a knock on my door. Fearghal Murphy informs me, 'We're on!' The news is that we'll fly out tonight. The plane is getting ready to go, so the bus will arrive shortly to pick us up for the airport.

'We're actually on!' I skip around the room, but stop short of jumping on the bed. *This is really happening.* I give Doug a quick emotional call. I tell him the news and he's as excited as I am. 'You've trained for this, now go and have fun. Remember, I'm with you all the way.' We part with 'I love you' and hang up.

I check-out of my room. The afternoon sun is still so bright and it's not long before I'm melting in my trousers. We have a group photo in front of the bus, and then we're off.

As we pull up near the runway, I catch a glimpse of the mighty Ilyushin plane. It has an incredible wingspan and several 'looking glass' windows beneath the nose. The Russian pilots must have the most amazing views of the frozen continent from there.

As I climb up the ladder to board, I'm reminded so much of the flight to the North Pole. There's a navigator at his desk at the front of the cabin, checking his dials and paperwork. There are rows of dark, vinyl seats and cargo cooped up in the netting behind. Cables hang in long loops from the ceiling and shafts of twilight spill in through the portholes.

I sit between Sarah and Stefan. We're all wearing our warm, bulky gear ready for the other end. I do up my safety belt and rest my head back against my seat. The engines roar, my heart beats wildly and somehow this massive plane races along the runway and lifts off. We're on our way, flying south. Four hours to Antarctica. Soon we'll touch down on ice.

At the front of the cabin there is a large bright screen with our flight tracking displayed, which makes for really interesting viewing. *Where have all the countries of the world gone?*

Our wheels eventually touch down, but it's a lot smoother than the North Pole, as it's more like an ice-skating rink with perfectly graded, glassy, glistening ice.

As the cabin door opens, I pull on my jacket and beanie and retrieve my red backpack from the spare seat. *It's time to go!*

Now there is something so special, so memorable, the moment you place your feet down in a place that you've dreamt about for months! I step off the ladder and out onto the ice. It's cold, but I'm more breathless from excitement than anything else, as this truly signifies the beginning of this marathon adventure.

The glacier is perfectly white, and above there's a pale blue sky. I believe it's the early hours of the morning, but honestly it could be anytime of the day or night. I'm still catching up on time zones and it's a mind-boggling 24-hour daylight here too.

We take some photos in front of the plane then bundle into several customised 4WD vehicles parked to the side of the runway. It's a short drive to camp and the steely blue rocks of the Ellsworth Mountain range rise up all around us.

Camp is quiet. Most staff are asleep. We're given a quick rundown of how the base operates and all the amenities, and then shown the fat-wheeled bikes we can hire if we feel the urge to exercise. *Really? Exercise?*

It's a well laid out base, with a communications tent, a mess tent, toilet block, shop, postbox, and rows of clamshell tents for sleeping, all perfectly aligned in the snow. The tents are named after explorers. Sarah and I share one called 'Palmer', which is named after Nathaniel Palmer, an American sea captain and explorer. It's not long before we tumble into bed.

## Wednesday, 20 January 2016

*Sarah and I sleep in for a little bit, but it's so bright, plus we're hungry, so we head to the mess tent for breakfast. It's an amazing blue-sky day and so dazzlingly on the ice. I'm thankful my mountaineering sunglasses are blocking out the glare.*

Through the first door there's an area to hang jackets and leave our boots. It's a smart buffer zone to keep the −20°C air outside. Through the second door, the warmth and sound of animated conversations hit us. It's busy in here. I look around the room—there are so many sunglass-tanned faces, so many people to talk with, and such an international mix. We fill up our plates with food and sit down.

After breakfast I wander over to watch them setting up the start/finish line gantry for the 100-kilometre ultra marathon, then I sit in on their race briefing. Tomorrow they'll be running 10 laps of the 10-kilometre circuit, and the race nutrition area will be set up here in the mess tent.

I write postcards to Doug, Bek and Cal, and post them in the little blue postbox sticking up out of the ice. Odds are I'll probably race these back to Australia, as I'll be home in about a week. I stamp the back page of my passport with the Union Glacier stamp, taking care to set the date to today. But as I press it down, the barrel flips and I end up with the 84 of July 2022. *Well, this just means I'll have to come back in 2022!*

It's time for a photo session in our race gear and then a few of us head off for a short training run to test out our gear. We go via the communications tent to sign out, and head out on the graded road.

I run with Sarah, Boon T Ong and Phing Ong, cousins from Singapore, and Hassan Baraka, a champion swimmer from Morocco. While there isn't the threat of polar bears like the

North Pole, there are crevasses, so we stick to the main road. Our turnaround point is an iconic little wooden Christmas tree at the road junction. It feels great to run. The crunch of the ice reminds me of the North Pole, but it's a firmer surface here because it's a glacier and not an icefloe, so it will be a whole lot kinder to my legs. It's milder here too, no where near −41°C!

It's been a great first day in Antarctica.

The next morning, I take my diary out and start writing:

### Thursday, 21 January 2016 – World Marathon Challenge 7.50am

*Slept well. More than five hours in a row for the first time in four days!*

*I'm feeling good. Settled. Happy.*

*So aware this is an incredible privilege to be here right now.*

*The Union Glacier is an immense white expanse surrounded by the rugged, snow-capped peaks of the Ellsworth Mountain range. The highest mountain in Antarctica, the Vinson Massif, is nestled somewhere in this long mountain range, reaching 4892 metres in altitude. The South Pole is only 1000 kilometres away.*

*The sun treks around in the sky all day and night. At 2am I woke up because it was so bright. I pulled my beanie down over my eyes. The wind has picked up overnight and the flags at the finish line are flying out. I love the sight of that Aussie flag! Had some great chats with people and loved getting to know Sarah and Stefan even better. Today the 100-kilometre race is going to be run. They'll start at 10am so I'll cheer them on and plan for our marathon.*

*Thank you to my mum and dad. They are the reason why*

*I am here. The World Marathon Challenge is a way I can continue their legacy in life.*

*I'm ready to go!*

*Life is an adventure, made complete with love, faith and joy.*

*I pray for strength, resilience, determination, hope and joy to run like the wind.*

*Live life to the full and live it amplified!*

The eight competitors for the 100-kilometre race line up together. I'm in awe of them. They've got a huge task ahead. Maybe one day I'll come back to try this one.

The starting hooter sounds and they're off. I cheer as they pull away from the start line and run off into the ice. Very soon they're tiny black dots in the distance.

I spend the rest of the day chatting with everyone from the WMC in the mess tent, and we punctuate our conversations to burst out of the tent to cheer on the 100-kilometre runners as they come past on another loop. It's exciting to think that this will be us soon. (But thankfully only 42 kilometres.)

The next morning I write in my diary again:

### Friday, 22 January 2016 – World Marathon Challenge 10.43am

*Yesterday we cheered on the runners in the 100-kilometre ultra race. They are all ages and abilities, and so inspirational. First place done in just over 12.5 hours, final competitor in approximately 24 hours. They all showed incredible resilience and perseverance. A timely message for us all as we are about to embark on our own race.*

*The weather is closing in with clouds covering most of the sky. It's a real contrast to yesterday's strong, bright sunshine and blue sky.*

*The plan is to start the race at 6.30pm today, and if the plane
is given the all clear to take off from Punta Arenas at 7pm, then
the message will come through to us while we're out on the course
to keep going, otherwise if the plane's postponed, we'll stop at
one lap and regroup for tomorrow. Race logistics are so dependent
on the elements, and this is such an extreme environment, things
can change dramatically. It's a matter of just going with the flow,
which is cool with me.*

*We had our race update this morning and were given a
start time. My heart was pounding. But I've come back to the
clamshell tent and laid out all my race gear and nutrition, and
I'm feeling a whole lot calmer. Because the weather is cooler, it's
made my decision a whole lot easier about what to wear. I'll wear
my black jacket, which has zipped ventilation sections on the
side and under the arms. It also has good-sized pockets (which
I've discovered!) for gels, snakes, so I can be self-sufficient and
not have to stop too much. I believe the wind is usually cooler
and stronger along the back stretch of the course, so I'll have my
balaclava and neck buff just in case. I'll have to choose between
ski goggles or glasses, but I'll work that out. I'll pin my teal
ovarian cancer ribbon onto my jacket now and put Mum's gold
wristwatch and Dad's folded handkerchief into the top pocket
next to my heart, and put on the orange wristbands for Can Too.
I'll have my surf lifesaving cap on top of my thin thermal beanie.*

*This is incredibly exciting to actually be starting the challenge,
after all these months of anticipation.*

*Today's race is dedicated to Mum and Dad, then additionally
to all surf lifesavers. I'll reflect on them all as I run. It will be
emotional, it will inspire me and it will encourage me along.*

*It's because of Mum and Dad that I'm here. They are my
inspiration, my motivation, my strength, my role models that I
measure myself with. They will run with me today.*

*All things are possible!*
*Ready to go …*
*The race is on!*

## 22 January 2016 – Marathon One – Antarctica

We start at 6.30pm under cloudy skies. It's an incredible moment, but we're still unsure whether this will be it or it will become a training run. Three kilometres in, a staff member from the base races up on a snowmobile and brings the news that we are all hoping for—the plane is on its way! *Excellent! The weather is going to hold, so we can keep running.*

My pace accelerates with my excitement. *So this is really it! We've officially started the World Marathon Challenge. Unreal!* I run past the little wooden Christmas tree and turn off from the road onto the back stretch. Here the mountains carry me along. The wind is cool, but not as blustery as I'd imagined.

It isn't long before my core starts heating up. I unzip my jacket, and then another kilometre on I resort to tying it around my waist. I run in my thermal top and wind shell pants for the remainder of the race.

Running in these dull conditions, as opposed to bright sunshine, makes it a lot more challenging and difficult to see the definition of dips and rises in the ice. The soles of my shoes shave the ice a number of times, so it's a matter of concentrating hard and trusting my feet. It feels so fabulous to turn the corner and see the base up ahead.

Lap one of four—a quick drink and energy gel and I'm off again. I feel good and my legs are handling the ice well. I keep a steady pace. I listen to my playlist of Midnight Oil, The Church, Icehouse, John Farnham, Paul Kelly … then halfway through this lap my phone freezes. *Not again!* So it's up to me to sing now. I also reflect on things. 'This race is for you, Mum and Dad!' I call out to the sky as I push along the back stretch.

Lap two of four—I have a drink from the aid station. But instead of getting back on the course, I race off to the bathroom.

Lap three of four is tough. I have gastro. It sweeps over me with such a violent urgency that within minutes I'm reduced to a shadow. I feel so sick and weak. I have pit stops with diarrhoea and I vomit twice. Fortunately there are perfectly placed facilities along the course. All up, I probably spend at least twenty minutes not running. Not ideal and certainly not a great position physically to be in for the first race. But each time I manage to sort myself out and soldier on. Besides, there's no way I'm quitting. I think back to all the training I've done, of what life has thrown at me. *Hey, I've been sicker than this before. I'm going to see this through. I'm determined …*

Towards the end of this lap, fortunately, I begin to feel better. I pick up my pace and overtake another competitor along the home stretch to the base.

Lap four of four—I revive! Only 10 kilometres to go! Out along the graded road and past the wooden Christmas tree. I try to make up for lost time. The clouds lean in on the mountains and the ice crunches beneath my shoes. There's a glimpse of blue sky along the horizon. My core is comfortable, my legs feel strong and I pull my buff up over my face to protect my upper lip from the cold. *This is what life is all about.*

'Pushing through, it's never perfect, but it can be made into being wonderful. Mum and Dad, you've run this with me. You are my heroes. To all the surf lifesavers, you make a world of difference to the beaches of Australia, and this is for you! For all your hours of volunteering, for the lives you've saved, for the sense of community that you build and for all the selfless service. You are my heroes too!'

I turn the final corner and stride out on the home stretch. Dan Cartica hands me the Australian flag and I cross the finish line waving it high.

In 5 hours, 18 minutes and 49 seconds, race number one of the World Marathon Challenge is done!

'Unreal!' I blurt out as usual. My upper lip is stiff and I sound posh and hilarious. Maybe I do talk like the queen after all.

Richard places the finisher's medal for Antarctica around my neck. I'm ecstatic! A cup of tea and almond biscuits go down so well. I sit in the mess tent for a few minutes and chat with those who've already finished. We are all so elated!

Stefan finishes and I help him warm up with a hot chocolate and some biscuits and gather some chairs and sit him in front of the heater. The relief to have this first race over is palpable. Everyone finishes under seven hours, so it's time to pack up our gear, load up the 4WDs and go.

We drive out along the road where we'd just run, and then off to the airstrip to board the Ilyushin aircraft. It's sitting there on the runway ready to fly. The blue sky has returned and all along the runway the ice glistens beautifully.

I take some last hurried photos as we shuffle single file towards the ladder. Then I take my final step on the ice. I'm sad to leave this incredible place, which I'd love to come back to, but right now it's time to race on with this adventure.

The plane streaks along the ice rink and we are off. 'Farewell Antarctica,' I murmur as we tilt towards the sky and turn to the north. I watch the navigator with his dials and gauges, and I listen to the roar of the engines. Everyone's quiet. I sip on water and doze and reflect on the race. There's only six to go. The next marathon will be later today, then that will mean, there'll only be five to go.

We touch down in Punta Arenas in the early morning light, and in steady rain. I wonder if we'll be running in this? For now, it's back to the hotel.

It's time for breakfast and a sleep.

## 23 January 2016 – Marathon Two – Punta Arenas

I put my race number on and pick up my bag that has all my race nutrition and drinks in it. It's time to gather in the foyer of the hotel and walk across to the beachfront promenade. I'm so relieved the rain has gone. It's sunny with light winds, and it feels like a completely different day. We group together for a photo with our country's flag, and James Alderson and I stand at the back to hold the Aussie one high. My legs are feeling quite stiff, but I'm hoping my hamstrings will loosen up as the race unfolds.

Moments later we bunch together at the start line, the hooter sounds and we're off. It's 4pm. The route is 8 laps of approximately 5 kilometres each. It's a wide footpath, slightly uphill, up and over a couple of footbridges, past some outdoor gym equipment and a carpark brimming with car enthusiasts and their pimped-up utes. The turnaround point is at a lookout, then it's back again to the start. Close by, the cool, deep waters of the Strait of Magellan stretch off to meet the eastern sky.

Everyone supports each other—there are plenty of encouraging words and high-fives as we pass. I start a tradition of aeroplane wings with my arms as I run past Phing and Boon, and Bob Weeks makes me laugh with his barking dog impersonation. A few laps in, he gives me the nickname Baby Puppy.

It's this camaraderie and sense of fun that's making this experience even more amazing. We're not alone and we're not here to compete and run each other off the track. Our team of fifteen is here for each other.

As the afternoon wears on, the sun is still bright and even though I'm wearing a singlet and shorts, I start to heat up. My mouth is so dry. It dawns on me I'm probably a little dehydrated from my gastro in Antarctica. I pick up a bottle of water from the aid station and clumsily drink it and run. I wish I'd thought about wearing my hands-free hydration pack. It's in my suitcase. I must get it out for Miami.

By lap four, my pace is slowing down. This second marathon is dedicated to Doug, Bek and Cal. I think of them individually, as well as all the experiences we've shared as a family. With Doug, it's our first date at the movies, our marriage at St Matthew's Anglican Church, starting our film business together, and all the swims at Coogee Beach and walks along the coastal path at sunset.

With Bek and Cal, it's their birth and their childhood years, the family get-togethers and the first run we did together at Centennial Park. I'm really looking forward to our next adventure that we've got planned—trekking 1700 kilometres along the Great Himalaya Trail in just under three weeks time.

On lap five, my thoughts of them continue to carry me through and I picture us getting our trekking boots on and breaking them in for Nepal. The sun is weakening and the wind is strengthening. The Strait of Magellan changes to a choppy, deepening blue. It's an incredible channel of water. At the distant port there's a cargo ship setting sail.

By lap six, I feel overwhelmingly tired and stop to sit on the stone wall at the turnaround point to put my head in my hands. The race official is quick to hand me his bottle of water.

I can't thank him enough. It gets me through this tough lap and back to the aid station.

Two laps to go.

Lap seven, I have a long drink of water and grab a couple of race gels to boost my energy levels. I'm so glad there's less than 10 kilometres to go now. At the turnaround point I smile broadly at the race official before running back into the wind.

Lap eight is the last lap. At last the day is cooling down. It's such a relief. I'm feeling better now so I pick up my pace and finish off strongly. I grab the finish tape and hold it with both hands across my body. *Hurray!*

In 4 hours, 47 minutes and 8 seconds, race number two of the World Marathon Challenge is done.

Richard hangs my finisher's medal for the South American continent around my neck. I have a massive piece of margherita pizza to celebrate, chat with Calum Ramm and wait to cheer for Sarah at the finish line.

I sleep so soundly and the next morning I make a number of visits to the breakfast buffet to add to my plate. I know I have to make the most of this because from here on things are going to pick up dramatically, as we race against the clock. We're going to be practically flying and running! It's going to be a matter of sleeping on the plane and eating at every opportunity. It's exciting but incredibly daunting at the same time. I've never done anything like this before.

The notorious winds of Punta Arenas play havoc as we check-in for our flight. It's no surprise that it's delayed. Normally I wouldn't be too fussed, but this is different, as we're on a very tight deadline. We wait nervously at the gate, stretching and rolling our legs and glancing at our watches.

We're told it's too windy to load the luggage because it will blow into the hold and potentially tip the plane over.

But minutes later the ground staff come up with an ingenious plan. They turn the plane around to face the cargo door away from the wind. *Clever!*

We board, with an hour lost from our stopover in Santiago. We'll be cutting it fine. Hopefully we can still make our connecting international flight to Miami.

We touch down and it's a race in itself to the baggage carousel, off to the check-in counter, sweating through the long line at security and then finding the gate. Everyone makes it. The World Marathon Challenge is still on!

I sleep and eat on the flight, then sleep some more. I pull on my recovery compression socks and they ease my aching feet and legs. I scribble a few scrawly, tired notes in my diary, and contemplate watching a movie, but doze off again. Eight hours, 44 minutes simply fly by ...

## 25 January 2016 – Marathon Three – Miami

Our plane touches down in Miami at 3.05am and soon we're into the terminal under bright fluorescent lights. I have trouble with the fingerprint scanner at security, for some reason my little fingers just don't seem to scan properly. I step aside and line up to see an officer. Everyone else goes through. I wonder if I'll encounter any problems.

So many flights in quick succession, a backpack bursting with sachets of race gels and white electrolyte powder ... I really hope I don't get mistaken for a drug runner. The line inches along and I do my best to keep my anxiousness under wraps. Finally I'm called forward, and I hand my passport over and smile. A couple of questions later, and my hands rescanned, my photo taken, my passport stamped and I'm free to go. *Sweet relief!*

I race to the carousel and find my suitcase doing lonely laps. Everyone's there and thankfully all our bags are too. Now it's time to change into our race gear in the terminal bathrooms. I choose my blue singlet and shorts for today, attach my race bib for Miami, spray anti-blistering product on my feet and fill up my hands-free hydration pack.

We drive to South Beach in two white vans. The lights of Miami are shining brightly. I gaze out the window and read the large traffic signs directing the far-off lanes from the freeway and into the suburbs. I check my watch and wonder what time it is back home.

When we pull into a carpark, it's still dark, so we stay warm in the vans, telling jokes, eating chocolate. I massage my calves and wiggle my feet around.

So here we are, marathon number three. We emerge from the van just as the first rays of sun light up the beachfront. The palm trees are spectacular. It's just how I imagined it would be.

Becca Pizzi's family introduce themselves to us, and their enthusiasm is infectious. I also meet Beth Ann Telford, a brain cancer survivor who will be running in the 2017 World Marathon Challenge. *What an amazing person.*

I get my headphones ready and walk towards the start line. We bunch together for our usual photo with our flags and then the hooter sounds and we're off! It's 7am.

The course follows a wide shipping channel lined with towering palm trees, and then it turns to pick up the coastal pathway parallel to Ocean Drive. On one side are art deco hotels with names like 'Starlite', 'The Tide', 'The Boulevarde', 'The Colony', while on the other is a white stretch of sand that dips its toes into a red, shimmering ocean.

*What a magnificent day.* With every lap I watch the progress of the beach staff setting up rows of deckchairs on the sand.

At times I'm swept along by buff-looking locals out for their fast morning jog.

I run a couple of laps with Hassan Baraka from Morocco. He's a champion ocean swimmer and is making the transition to marathon running with incredible ease. *Impressive!*

Several people have flown in to support us today. There's 'Team Jonny', which includes Jonny Wade's parents. They're here to support Pat Fallon today, who's raising funds for cancer research in memory of their young son, Jonny. I stop and give them a hug. I can't help but cry. It must be absolutely heartbreaking to lose a child.

There's also friends, Karen Curtis and Gloria Lau, from the North Pole marathon. Also at the start/finish line is Alvin Matthews, a marathon runner who'd had a devastating accident last year and is now a paraplegic. I give him a hug and tell him I'll be back, and then I'm off again beneath the palm trees.

I dedicate today to my brothers, Trevor and Ray, and my extended family. I go through them one by one. I love them all dearly. My mind also drifts back to 1969, when we travelled here with our little dot of a caravan and Chevrolet. I'm sure the retro hotels would have looked just the same and there would be deckchairs on the sand too. I love this whole concept of retracing footsteps from all those years ago.

I take regular sips of electrolyte fluid from my pack and break open another race gel. The morning's heating up but I'm coping a whole lot better than in Punta Arenas. This strategy is working.

'Come on, Heather,' I tell myself, 'only four laps to go.'

A song comes on my playlist. It's 'Dancing on the Ceiling', by Lionel Richie. *Love it!* I press the repeat button on my headphone cable over and over again. It's a perfect song for this location.

At last I'm onto the final lap. As I pass Sarah, I give her an extra special hug and I make funny, floppy aeroplane wings with Phing and Boon to indicate how tired I'm getting now. I race beneath the palm trees one last time, and cross the finish line to say, 'Unreal!'

Richard Donovan presents me with my finisher's medal for the North American continent. *Fantastic!*

In 4 hours, 46 minutes and 12 seconds, race number three of the World Marathon Challenge is done.

I thank Richard tearfully and then take a few steps over to Alvin. I quietly take the medal from my neck and lay it gently around his. He is on a far more difficult journey than what I'll ever face running these marathons. I embrace him and sit down next to his wheelchair and sob.

A short time later Richard Donovan gives me a spare medal. 'What you just did was a really lovely gesture. You deserve a complete set, Heather,' he says gently.

I'm so humbled and grateful.

Before we know it, we're back in the white vans heading along the freeway to the international airport. The buildings and signs flash by. Very soon we'll be off on a plane to Madrid.

## 26 January 2016 – Marathon Four – Madrid

It's becoming a pattern now of sleeping and eating on the plane, writing in my diary and dozing. It's eight hours until touch down and it will be Australia Day morning when we arrive in Madrid.

All our bags arrive and we change in the airport bathrooms. I'm getting better at this and it's helpful when there's more than one hook on the back of the toilet door. We climb aboard a coach and we're off to weave through the chaotic city traffic and arrive at the Casa de Campo Park in Central Madrid. We're a touch behind schedule, so the plan is to get started as soon as we can after our briefing and a quick photo with the flags.

I apply some sunscreen, sip from my hydration pack, and put on my sunglasses. Fortunately the temperature is cool, but not too cold.

Several runners from last year's World Marathon Challenge are here to support us. They are awesome and spread themselves out among us at the start line. The hooter sounds and we're off. We run and chat. There's such a strong bond, which is not surprising, because out of the whole world right now, they are the only ones who know exactly what we're going through!

The Madrid course is eight laps along tree-lined roads up a long hill and back. At this time of the morning the park is quiet. It's a really beautiful, peaceful place.

After lap three, the gradual gradient begins to take its toll. My legs are definitely feeling tired today and I can tell my muscle reserves are getting low. I resign myself to the fact that it's going to be a challenge today—it's just a matter of getting through it.

I get some relief going back down the hill, but turning and running back up is a slog.

At the halfway mark, I'm craving something to give me a boost. I sit down at the aid station and sip some soft drink.

As I chat with the staff it occurs to me that this is actually the halfway mark of the entire World Marathon Challenge. Anything beyond this point is on the home stretch. This is a landmark moment and I can feel the excitement rising up inside. All I need to do is run the same amount again. I finish my cup and I get up and run!

This marathon is dedicated to all my friends in life—young, old, from years ago and today. My school friends, friends from youth group, nursing, and the Surf Lifesaving Club. I think about the warmth, the richness and colour that they've added to my life and I'm so grateful for their love, support, advice and companionship throughout the past fifty years. They help to get me through the final laps.

As the sun begins to sink, the Spanish air becomes chillier. At last I can see the finish line ahead. I'm so happy. I'm nearly there! I take off my sunglasses to wipe my eyes and look up at the trees. However, this momentary lapse in concentration is costly … there's a tree root sticking up on the path ahead. My right foot clips the top and I have no time to react, and so I stumble forward with arms outstretched and hit the dirt. I'm winded and shocked.

I can't believe what I've just done. Beads of blood appear on the heels of my hands and there are grazes on my elbows and knees. But I can't just lay here. So I pick myself up, pull myself together and run on to the finish line.

In 5 hours, 3 minutes and 41 seconds, race number four of the World Marathon Challenge is done.

I sit in the same chair that I rested in earlier and the aid station staff clean and dress my wounds. Their kindness and gentleness makes me crumple inside. I feel foolish and vulnerable. I've really let myself down and I simply can't stop the tears rolling down my cheeks. I thank them and quietly gather up my gear and head to the backseat of the bus where I curl up and sob. I'm so glad no one else is on the bus to see this. I'm absolutely shattered.

I really didn't need this right now because the Morocco marathon is only a few hours away. It's the shortest turnaround time between all the races and I wonder how I'm going to run feeling like this. I'm aching and bruised and exhausted. This is my lowest point of the entire race so far. *What am I going to do?*

As the other competitors load onto the bus and give me hugs, I begin to settle. I start to refocus on being positive. It could have been a whole lot worse than this—true. I have five hours until the next marathon to rest—that's a good thing. I am not alone—that's another good point. I've got some paracetemol and chocolate—perfect.

I feel more determined to pick myself up from here, and I vow that no matter how sore I am at the start line in Marrakesh, I'll run until I can't run anymore and then I'll walk to the finish line from there.

The bus engine is running, as Sarah bravely finishes her run, and we race to the airport to catch the plane. We make it to our gate with minutes to spare and settle into our seats in our sweaty running gear. It's a brief flight, only two hours, and soon we're touching down on our next continent—Africa.

## 27 January 2016 – Marathon Five – Marrakesh

It's pushing on 10pm as I watch the luggage spin around the carousel at Marrakesh airport. It's kind of mind-numbing and my eyes are increasingly tired as I study the big black suitcases rumbling past. *But where's mine?*

One by one everyone else retrieves their luggage. *Surely it couldn't have got lost on the shortest flight of the entire trip?* I walk anxiously away to the other side of the carousel and find a pile of luggage that's slipped off a sharp turn. *Sweet relief, it's here!*

At this time of night the airport is quiet, and as we wait for our bus we stretch and pace, tell jokes and take 'selfies'. Pat uses a roller on his sore, tight leg muscles.

It's a beautiful, mild evening. Very soon we're at our hotel, nestled in among some magnificent gardens of spotlit date palms. It's our brief base for this leg of the journey.

It feels so good to change into fresh running gear and I shove my dirty clothes into my laundry bag, which is now taking over my suitcase. I open my medical kit and take a few more paracetamols to ease my throbbing hands and knees, and I secure the dressings on my hands with extra lengths of tape. I clip on the race bib for Morocco. Here we go …

It's edging on midnight as we gather at the city square. Mohamad Ahansal, the Moroccan ultra marathon champion, is here and he welcomes us warmly, along with the Marrakesh media. Mohamad is such a humble champion and he'll be staying up all night manning our aid station and giving us encouragement. *What a legend!*

I do a brief TV interview, forgetting that I have my headphones in the whole time—*oh dear … how tired am I?*

So this is marathon number five, the one we've all been worried about the most. The reasons being that it's so soon after Madrid, we'll be running through the night, and there's now accumulated fatigue in our legs from the other four marathons.

But as I stand at the start line, I tell myself that it's going to be okay. This is the essence of what life and what this World Marathon Challenge is all about: it's rising to challenges, pushing through, supporting each other, getting to the finish line, and achieving seemingly impossible dreams.

The starting hooter sounds, and by the time we round the first corner on the pavement, we've spread out into a long single file. The course skirts around the city square. On the inside it's filled with date palms and dromedaries, and it's quiet, and on the outside there's just the odd motorcycle and taxi going past. Several police watch over us, and while the city sleeps, we run on into the wee small hours of the night.

I track well, despite my grazed knees and throbbing hands, and I dedicate this marathon to the future, to faith, to life. I'm so grateful be alive, and so thankful that my ovarian cancer was caught in time. I want to help spread awareness of its signs and symptoms, and encourage people to act on them. I also want to keep raising funds for cancer research. I picture my mum and dad running beside me, shoulder to shoulder, encouraging me along.

The Bee Gees are next on my playlist with 'Stayin' Alive', and I smile and slip a little boogie or two into my running style—lap three is memorable!

I push on around the city square. 'Nutbush City Limits' by Tina Turner and 'Beds are Burning' by Midnight Oil help me run through laps five and six, and gradually the kilometres melt away.

On my final lap, dawn is not far away. I pick up my speed around the final corner in the pavement and cross over the finish line. Mohamad Ahansal places my finisher's medal around my neck and we stand together to have a photo and a chat. He's such a gentle hero and I thank him for looking after us.

I do a quick interview with Dave Painter, our video cameraman, and start out completely composed, by saying, 'I am so, so grateful to be alive ...' However, within seconds I'm choked up with tears. This race has been emotionally profound. I know I'll look back on this one, and even though it was one of the hardest, it will definitely be one of my favourites because I didn't run this one alone.

In 5 hours, 3 minutes and 44 seconds, race number five of the World Marathon Challenge is done.

Now there's only two to go.

I stay for fifteen minutes more, and then I climb onto the shuttle bus to head back to the hotel. I peel off my bandages and stand under the shower and let my weariness and sweat and tears wash away. I eat a handful of biscuits and have an hour's rest on the large, soft bed.

Then we're all back on the bus heading to the airport. It's morning peak hour and the airport is a completely different place. We battle our way through the crowds and board a domestic flight to Casablanca. I have very little recollection of this flight, as I sleep the whole way.

## 28 January 2016 – Marathon Six – Dubai

It's the early hours of the morning, and from the bus window all the bright lights and skyscrapers of Dubai dazzle like a futuristic movie set. We check into another hotel for a brief few hours and catch the lift up among the man-made treetops.

Sarah and I share a room and it's wonderful to chat, have a cup of tea, have one of my rehydrated meals and set the alarm for at least two hours sleep. Sarah tends to her blisters and puts ice on her swollen ankle. I'm so inspired by her willpower, she's clearly in a lot of discomfort, but she still keeps going.

At breakfast, in the downstairs restaurant, we bump into James, Demelza and Dave. 'Two marathons to go!' we say happily, and there's talk about our 'war wounds'.

Minutes later we're storing our luggage and on our way to the marathon route. In the daylight, I get a better sense of the enormity of this place. There are entire city blocks of construction work dedicated to building even taller towers.

As our bus pulls in to the beachfront, I see Suzie Simonian, the sister of my next-door neighbor, Jo Smith. She's holding up a sign. *How wonderful to see a familiar face.* I race off the bus and into a great big hug.

Today's marathon is dedicated to all those with ovarian cancer, to those who've been lost, to those who are fighting hard, to all those beautiful ladies with heartbreaking diagnoses who I met in hospital waiting rooms. I grasp my teal ribbon tightly and spend a moment gazing out at the vast 'teal' sea. It's the perfect colour for today. A quick photo with our flags, then it's on with marathon number six!

Our course follows a curving pathway along the Dubai beachfront. A fresh coastal breeze is blowing, keeping the air temperature in the low twenties and sending the colourful windsurfers and kitesurfers skimming across the sea. They're a great distraction from my stiff, shuffling legs.

It's a tough race, with fatigue and old injuries starting to show among many of the competitors. We call out extra words of encouragement and keep soldiering on. My friend Suzie runs a lap with me, and at about the halfway mark I run and chat with Demelza too.

On the second-last lap, I'm totally spent, and sit on the esky at the turnaround point. I tell the support staff they are fabulous people and munch on salty potato chips and sip some soft drink. It's definitely not the healthiest snack, but it gives me the boost I need. I get up and head back to the start/finish line. I've got one more loop to run.

'So this is it,' I tell myself, 'there's only a handful of kilo-metres to go.' I stride out with the kitesurfers in my sights and with the ovarian cancer survivors in my heart.

The wind dries up my sweat as soon as it appears on my face. *Faster, faster...* I will my legs along. Around a couple of final curves, then I'm there at last.

In 5 hours, 18 minutes and 48 seconds, race number six of the World Marathon is done.

Back at the hotel we have a couple of hours rest, to shower and eat pizzas before heading off to the airport. But this flight feels different, as I'm going home!

## 29 January 2016 – Marathon Seven – Sydney

About an hour out of Sydney, I open up my diary and write:

*Ate and slept on the plane. My heart is full. I'm so happy knowing that there's only one marathon to go, but so sad to be leaving everyone at the finish line. They are such awesome friends and we've shared so much and bonded so closely. Tears well up when I think about saying goodbye to them all, especially Sarah.*

*Sarah and I had an early morning coffee together in the lounge area, and chatted and raised our coffee cups in a toast to 'life'.*

*This has been such an incredible journey.*

*I'm nearly home, now it's time to finish this challenge.*

I pack everything away in my red backpack and into the pockets of my jacket. I give TG the Bear a hug and sit quietly in my seat.

The tyres touch the runway and the engines roar. But this time there's no ice to land on, no powerful winds, no other connecting flights to catch. This is the final stop for me, the last runway on this epic journey … I'm home, with just one more job to do.

I turn my mobile phone on. It's back in service and filled with wonderful messages.

Our luggage appears quickly on the carousel and we bundle onto the bus. It's late Friday night. The roads are wet and the city lights are twinkling—a thunderstorm has just swept through.

As we drive across the Cahill Expressway, the Opera House glows gently against the dark waters of the harbour. I gaze out at its beautiful white sails. *To think that this is the place where I've run to so many times in training. Where I dreamt of the WMC … and here I am tonight, about to fulfill this personal dream.*

As the bus starts out across the Harbour Bridge, I look up at the spotlit pylons and majestic arches and have a moment of incredible clarity. It's a very special moment. For right now the profound impact that running has had on my life is truly hitting home. Tonight I'll have the opportunity to pull something off that is so extreme and so unbelievable and would've been completely impossible only four short years ago. I'm elated, excited and my spirits soar.

We arrive in Manly and pull in at the Novotel. I methodically put on my race gear for the very last time. I'm wearing my orange Can Too Foundation singlet along with my surf lifesaving cap. I tuck my hair up into a messy bun, clip my race bib on and put my race nutrition into my bag. *I'm ready.* It's the last marathon, and my anticipation levels are sky high. I'm so happy. In a few minutes time I'll be seeing my family and friends.

In the foyer I meet Fran Seton and Dave Cundy for the first time. Dave is the Vice President and Technical Director of the Association of International Marathons and Distance Races (AIMS), and has measured the course here at Manly Beach.

We have a quick race briefing then head to Manly Surf Lifesaving Club. We pass the restaurant strip with its loud music and busy bars—people are having a normal, fun Friday night.

We cross the road and I see my family for the first time. Doug, Cal, Bek and Matt—my family is all here, and I couldn't be happier facing up to this final race.

My brothers and my niece, Hannah, and nephew, Pete, and his girlfriend, Lauren are all here too, as are my cousins, Alison and Kelly, and my neighbours and friends from Can Too. *Wow! How beautiful to see them all.* I hug everyone several times over.

I'm so grateful for their belief in me and for their incredible support. There's only 42.195 kilometres to go tonight—we can do this together.

We gather for one last pre-race photo behind the World Marathon Challenge banner. Then we all line up at the start line. *Ready? Let's go!*

The lights along Manly promenade stretch out in front and I can feel the ocean breeze on my face. It's a wonderful flat course to North Steyne Surf Lifesaving Club and back. Cal, Pete and Lauren take turns riding bikes behind me. Hannah is on her skateboard and Matt and Bek run some laps with me too. They also spin off to support other runners too. *This is awesome.* I'm so proud of them. My good friend, Glenn Duffus, appears to take photos and Pete captures some too.

Each time I complete a lap there are more and more supporters cheering us on. They spread out along the promenade, sitting on the park benches, leaning against the sea wall, holding up signs and giving high-fives as we run past. Keith Hong, another good friend, is at the turnaround point and his 'neon light' smile spurs me on.

One by one the laps clock over. I count them and tick them off the list in my head. By the time lap six arrives, a sickening exhaustion is creeping into my legs. The past six marathons are taking their toll. I run with a bag of potato chips in one hand and a race gel in the other. I tell myself to keep on going … and fortunately I soon feel better.

It's well after midnight and even more support arrives: my friends from the Surf Lifesaving Club, friends from the Salvos, neighbours, and even my friends from the Coogee Cougars running group run a lap with me. *This is absolutely awesome!* I'm so blown away by their encouragement and this really spurs me on.

As I pass the 4 hour, 15 minute mark, I start on my final lap. Cal rides beside me on his bike. It's just the two of us. The sea breeze is blowing gently and there are some distant ships out to sea. I turn the far marker and head for home.

So much is going on inside my heart and it spills out in waves of words. 'Hey, Cal. Always live life to the full, always push the boundaries and never give up on your dreams. Anything is possible. This is an incredible moment in our lives right now … Let's celebrate!'

Cal and I shout one word out at the ocean together—'Unreal'

The promenade lights curve us towards the finish line. My friends are forming a guard of honour there. I'm given an Aussie flag and I race beneath the canopy of outstretched hands. I catch sight of the ribbon at the end. It's getting closer. I'm nearly there.

Then … at last … I am.

In 4 hours, 39 minutes and 21 seconds, race number seven of the World Marathon is done.

'Unreal!'

Incredible relief washes over me, and joy bursts up and plants a smile on my face as wide as my mouth can handle. I hug my family and disappear into their arms. Then I hug my brothers and everyone else!

Richard Donovan presents me my finisher's medals—one for the Australian continent and another for completing the World

Marathon Challenge. I can't thank him enough for granting me this privilege to do something so life-changing as this.

Doug wraps me up in a jacket and towel and I sip on some water. I cheer the others coming in, especially Sarah. I am so happy that she's done it too.

I'm tired but don't feel like sleeping. My legs shake with adrenaline and exhaustion.

At 5am I find a quiet place inside the surf club to talk to ABC radio. So much comes spilling out and I'm relieved I'm able to string words together and sound reasonably cohesive!

The sky lightens in the east—morning is here. Soon the sun will rise on one of the best days of my life.

Later that morning, everyone gathers for one last walk and photo together along Manly promenade. This time we're not in running gear, and there are no flags, no start/finish line gantry. We're simply a bunch of close friends standing arm in arm, laughing and smiling.

If I could just freeze time here … to stay a little longer. Spend the day. But I have to go. I've committed to a couple of television interviews on the other side of the harbour.

But how do you say goodbye to friends who have been through so much with you? It's incredibly hard. Words such as 'thank you so much', 'come and visit', 'let's run another event together', and 'catch you on Facebook' don't quite sum up how we're feeling inside, and it's our silent hugs that actually translate it better.

I turn away in tears and walk down Manly Corso to the ferry terminal, alone.

On the timetable the next ferry is scheduled in five minutes. I race to buy a ticket and walk up the gangplank and sit inside on the lower deck. I watch as the deckhands free the ropes from the wharf. The engines rumble and the water churns as we pull away and the ferry starts back on its regular trip to Circular Quay.

I sit with my red backpack on my knees. It's filled with my running gear, medals, TG the Bear and my colourful diary. I'm in among the Saturday morning crowds to the city, lost in everything that's so perfectly normal.

We sail past the Sydney Harbour heads, and there's the gentle rock from the moving tide. Up ahead the Opera House tiles shine brightly in the summer sun. All around me is a busy, sparkling harbour, and a blue, cloudless sky.

I only have a few more minutes left to myself, so I reach into my backpack for my diary and write:

### Saturday, 30 January 2016

*These past seven days have been the culmination of my life so far, and as the bow wave from the ferry spills away and sends some little boats bobbing, I can't help but think about the truth in all of this.*

*Inside I am the same old me: the shy curly-haired ten year old who froze at the thought of giving school speeches; the fifteen-year-old teenager who was told she was ugly and uncool by school bullies; the twenty-one-year-old nurse who mapped out an outback adventure; the thirty-year-old mother who survived sleep-deprived nights with a colicky baby and a toddler, and dreamed of writing children's books; the forty-year-old daughter who cradled her mother as she battled a stroke; the forty-one-year-old wife with ovarian cancer; the forty-seven-year-old Aussie who went running in her crinkled, old gardening shorts.*

*I'm me, the same old me. And inside, all these familiar people are still there, still tucked away, but today I have one more to add. One more person that will paint sunshine on my soul.*

*I'm the fifty-year-old adventurous spirit who learnt that anything is possible if you keep believing, if you stare down your fears, stand at the start line and dare yourself to go.*

*As the ferry pulls in to Circular Quay, tears roll down my cheeks. I know that for now my journey is complete.*

Thanks to the support of family and friends in those seven crazy days. I raised close to $15,000 for cancer research through the Can Too foundation to fund researchers. This made me so excited, and I would do it all again in a heartbeat, if I could raise even more to help save lives.

# Chapter Eleven

# MOUNTAINS, VALLEYS AND MUM

## *The Great Himalaya Trail*

## 2016

It's the 21 April 2016, Day 54 of the Great Himalaya Trail, and Cal, Bek, Matt and I are about a third of the way through our epic journey across Nepal. Tonight finds us camped out with our Nepalese team on a broad rocky plateau. We're curled up in the lap of a magnificent mountain pass called Renjo La.

Tomorrow we'll be climbing up it's steep, switchback trail, and reaching an airless altitude of 5340 metres. From there we'll head further west, down into a long, dusty valley to Thame and on towards the Tibetan border—trekking for another 97 days!

Far below us the tiny, bright lights of Gokyo village twinkle and swim in the turquoise waters of the lake. It's hard to believe that we were all the way down there last night, tucked up in a teahouse, sleeping beneath a corrugated iron roof, with windows and floral curtains, in a real wooden bed!

But as comfortable as that was, there's no place like this plateau tonight, for here I am, leaning out of my little yellow tent, cocooned in my sleeping bag, watching the most amazing theatre production on earth.

Over Everest, a full moon is rising and the clouds have cleared just in time, letting it spill its silvery lunar light across the peaks. Across the skyline, the sleeping giants of the Himalayas are bathed in a timelessness and a magnificence like no other place on earth.

Everest is wearing its signature plume and it feathers out to the south, wrapping Lhotse's peak up for the night in a long, gentle sheet of white. I can't help but think of my mum, she would have loved it here, for out of everyone in our family, she loved the mountains the most.

I stay awake for another thirty minutes or so, but around 9.30pm, the clouds return and the 'curtains close'. I zip up my tent and drift off to sleep on a Himalaya high.

A few hours later, I hear footsteps and have a feeling they are Cal's. I wriggle out of my sleeping bag and peer out to see his tall, silhouetted frame and head torch moving around near his tent. It's still dark; he shouldn't be up at this time, well, not up for this long at least. *Something must be wrong.*

I pull on my boots, jacket and gloves and scramble over the rocks to get to him.

As I get closer I can see he's shaking uncontrollably in the cold … and vomiting. My spirits plummet. Gastro is terrible at the best of times, but at altitude it completely wipes you out.

*If only it could be me*, I think to myself, as any mother would, and support him around the shoulders. *I'd swap places right now, no questions asked.*

I return to my tent to grab my medical kit, and help Cal back into his sleeping bag. He's so nauseous and cold. I give him stemetil and we sit together in the doorway of his tent. The air is icy, and although it chills my face, I'm not leaving his side, not even for a minute.

Fortunately for us, the kitchen team is stirring for an early start. Our Nepalese guide, Juddha Rai, comes over to check on us. Within minutes he's organised hot water bottles and we position these around Cal's body. Juddha stays with us. I'm not sure how long we're here, but the eastern sky begins to pale to a transparent blue. Dawn is here. It's Day 55 of our trek.

We watch as the first rays shoot up into the sky, they're like searchlights to heaven. Everest's plume is backlit and golden, and my beloved Makalu, my first favourite mountain on this trek, comes back into view. Behind us the sunlight skips across the peaks. It checks them off in order of height, then runs down the ridge lines to shine on our faces. We close our eyes, and soak up its warmth.

Right now I'm a muddle of emotions. Elated to be in this place, but incredibly tired and worried. Is Cal going to make it over Renjo La?

At 6.30am we begin to slowly pack up camp and have breakfast. We divide the contents of Cal's backpack up among us, and then set off. Tsering Lama stays a few steps in front of Cal, while Bek, Matt and I follow closely behind. Juddha walks watchfully at the rear.

There's no shade, not a scrap of vegetation on this shale, rocky landscape, and the sun keeps us in full view as we battle the switchbacks to the pass.

Cal stops frequently to rest on the rocks, sometimes to dry retch, other times to sip his hydrolyte. He's doing it tough, but he doesn't complain, he soldiers on and we help him as best as we can.

Below us, the grey boulder-strewn Ngozumpa Glacier carves its way between the stone feet of the peaks. Further up the path we peel off our jackets and reapply invisible zinc on our sweaty cheeks. Cal manages to keep down a dry biscuit or two and takes longer sips from his water bottle. It's an encouraging sign.

Soon we're scrambling in among large boulders, and pushing up into the final 100 metres to the pass. It's hard, breathless work, and I resort to counting steps, just like I did at the Amphu Labtsa pass. I get to 100, then go back to one.

Thirty minutes later the colourful prayer flags of Renjo La reach out to welcome us in. We have a family hug to celebrate and our Sherpas join in too.

Tsering Lama kneels to light incense and chants, 'Om Mani Padme Hum.'

We lower our heads and let his words weave around us. It's wonderful. I can feel the stress melting away. I know Cal's not out of the woods yet, but at least he's made it through the toughest part of the day. It's downhill to camp from here.

At the top of the pass is a long rocky ledge, so we peel off our backpacks and sit with our Nepalese team and gaze out at the view. It's absolutely awesome. I feel like we're picking up again from where we left off at dawn—there's the mountains, Everest's plume, Gokyo Lake, and the vast blue sky.

An hour passes … and it's obvious no one wants to be the first to leave. But camp is still several hours away, and we really have to go. Our porters and kitchen staff pick up their loads, then Tsering Lama and Lackpa Sherpa, and then Cal, Bek and Matt follow them closely behind.

I hoist my backpack reluctantly onto my shoulders, and

take one final, lingering look. I'm trying my best to memorise the skyline, because this will probably be the last time I see it with my very own eyes.

'Farewell Makalu, Lhotse, Lobuche, Nuptse, and Cholatse. Farewell Everest …' I murmur.

Mum would have really loved these mountains. Just like her favourite ones: Cradle Mountain, Mount Sonder, Mount Donna Buang and Mount Dandenong.

I turn to follow the others.

The trail descends away quickly from the high pass, into a series of steep sandstone steps. They disappear into the shadows, taking me quickly into the valley below.

I'm tired and emotional, and for the first time in a long while, I find myself walking on my own. I think about the mountains and I think about my mum—my beautiful, angelic Mum, and before I know it my thoughts are tumbling away, back to the night that my family walked down into the longest, deepest 'valley' of our lives, back to Monday, 21 March 2005 …

A fine rain is falling as the ambulance drives down our long gravel driveway and turns left onto Canterbury Road, Melbourne. Mum and I have driven this way so many times together over the past thirty-two years. But tonight is so devastatingly different.

Even though we haven't reached the hospital yet, I know the diagnosis. Mum has had a massive stroke. I turn frequently from the passenger seat to watch the paramedic tend to her. I'm desperate to help. *If only there's something I can do...*

Soon we're approaching our first intersection, the siren wails, and we race through the red traffic lights. Dad and Ray are following along somewhere behind us in Dad's car.

Right now Mum's life hangs in the balance. She's ashen, barely responsive and looking so unfamiliarly fragile in her favourite pale blue nightie. The paramedic works desperately to clear her airway—he repositions her, and then suctions her mouth again. He places her on oxygen and gently cradles her head. It's incredibly distressing to watch, but I can't look away. I have to stay with her. I need to keep her in my sights otherwise she might slip away.

Another intersection, another red light, the siren wails on wildly. We have another fifteen minutes to go. *Come on. Come on. We have to hurry.* I answer some questions so the paramedics have a better idea of Mum's health history, and the events leading up to tonight. But my voice is so strained and high, it doesn't sound like me. There's no disguising that I'm shattering inside.

This is my mum we're talking about—my foundation, my very first best friend, my gentlest, dearest companion, the axis of my world, and the centre of our family's universe.

The ambulance arrives at Accident and Emergency and Mum's quickly assessed and stabilised. Dad and Ray arrive shortly after.

They race her to radiology for a CT scan to check what's happened—is it a clot or a bleed on her brain? She's on warfarin, a blood thinner, so it could be either.

While she's gone, we field a thousand questions from the medical staff and answer them as best we can. But inside my head only one question rises up. It's one word, and I want to yell it out at the whole wide world right now—*WHY?*

My brother, Trevor, arrives and we all wait together in the tiny, airless hospital lounge. Dad is inconsolable. We hold him tightly. We've shared so many experiences as a family, but nothing like this. This is such unfamiliar, distressing territory, and it's out of our control. We huddle and cry, talk in questions, sit in silence, hold each other, pray and wait.

I walk briefly outside into the dawn light to call Doug. I'm not even sure what I say to him, and then I return to the lounge to wait.

Mum is wheeled back and her results confirm it's a massive clot and she is not expected to live. *What?* Dad, Trevor, Ray and I are sent reeling from one devastating blow to another. All they can do, they say, is make her as comfortable as possible, and all we can do, they recommend, is prepare ourselves for the impossible task of saying goodbye.

But Mum is only seventy-three years old.

We sit by her bedside taking turns to hold her hands and telling her how much we love her. I caress Mum's forehead and smooth her beautiful white curls with my fingers. She opens her eyes. I know she recognises us all. I know she knows what's going on, but she just can't tell us … she can't speak … the stroke has affected her speech. More than that, her beautiful face is drooping on the left, and the entire right side of her body is paralysed.

This hurts so much to see the most angelic, perfect person on this earth lying here, broken in pieces.

Our morning blurs into the afternoon, the night into the next morning. Mum's transferred from Accident and Emergency, and into the ward. She keeps hanging onto life.

We gather chairs from wherever we can and sit next to her bed. We stay by her side and we don't let her hands go.

Mum's room is soon filled with flowers and cards from her friends, neighbours and extended family. It's an incredible outpouring of love. We share the flowers, and this love, with the rest of the ward.

Over the coming days, Mum regains some cognitive alertness and physical strength, but she has suffered extensive brain damage, which means her speech has permanently gone and the paralysis will remain. It's devastating, but she will survive and for that we are really grateful.

She begins to sit out of bed and becomes more aware of her surroundings. Her ability to swallow improves and she progresses from fluids to puree foods. It's a massive learning curve back into life, but she tries as hard as she possibly can. It's this determination that I've always loved about her and I know it's this determination that will get her through.

Easter comes and goes. We spend as much time as possible helping with Mum's personal care and doing additional exercises to reduce muscle wasting and to prevent contractures in her affected limbs. We bring in books and music and jigsaw puzzles. We read to her, reminisce, and often sit in silence just keeping her company. There are little victories and setbacks. I really miss hearing her voice, and having our mother–daughter chats. She's still here, but it's different.

Discussions begin with the doctors as to what the future holds.

I celebrate my 40th birthday with a chocolate cake, and Mum and I pose for a photo. We put on party hats and have a moment of joy. She tries her best to smile and I put on a brave face. This lasting image captures everything.

I head home to Sydney for a few days to catch up with family and to take care of some work responsibilities. It's all a blur. Doug's managing to keep life and soul together here, running our business and looking after Bek and Cal. His strength is incredible, and I can't thank him enough for getting our family through this time. A few days later I head back down to Melbourne.

Mum moves from hospital into a rehabilitation facility for eight-weeks intensive therapy. She's fitted with a leg brace and learns to take her first steps again on her numb, buckling leg. She concentrates hard in between the parallel bars and a few weeks later progresses to a walking frame. Her fighting spirit shines through and we are all so proud of her. She has sessions with an occupational therapist to attempt to relearn daily skills, and a speech therapist to find ways to communicate. We see some improvements, but Mum still has such a long way to go.

Then we receive difficult news from the doctors. This is probably the extent of her recovery. Nothing more can be done for her here, she will need to be placed into a nursing home. But Dad refuses to accept this. 'Please let me take Elva home.'

A week later, and against all the odds, Dad brings Mum home to stay. His is a love so overwhelmingly deep and true. We are all so proud of him.

Dad enables Mum to pick up the colours of life again, to look out at her familiar purple mountains at sunset and to walk in their garden with her frame.

They go to church, take her motorised wheelchair along walking trails at Warburton, they shop and live life to the full as best they can. Trevor, Ray and I help him, and we stay often, together as a family.

Mum and Dad spend a Christmas here in Sydney and they fly to Alice Springs for a winter holiday and hire a 4WD to explore the Finke River and Rainbow Valley, just like old times, with a few adaptions.

Then just when we feel like some stability has returned to our world, February 2007 arrives and so does my ovarian cancer. How much more can one family possibly take? We're already stretched to our emotional limits.

I'm absolutely gutted, aware that it's going to take me out of the equation of caring for Mum for the moment, and knowing that it's going to hit them hard. Parents never stop being parents, and equally, as their child, the last thing I want to do is bring them both grief.

Doug helps me to make the phone call and we speak with Dad first, he then holds the receiver up for Mum. I can hear her breathing. She makes sounds, as she's desperately trying to form words, doing her very best to comfort me. My tears fall uncontrollably into my lap as I picture her on the other end of the phone.

But as bleak as things may seem right now, there still is light. For Mum has thrown me a lifeline. Even though she hasn't uttered a word tonight, it's by her being the way she is, for all those forty-one years of life as mother and daughter, she has actually shown me the way through from here. I'm not going to be angry; I'm not going to fall apart. I am going to be strong, determined and positive. She has taught me well. I will plan to survive.

Four weeks after my surgery I fly down to see them and hug them both so tightly. It's an incredibly emotional reunion. I'm still weak, and have trouble pushing Mum's wheelchair when we're out shopping, and I strain my abdomen lifting her in and out of bed, but apart from that, we pick up again where we left off.

Then on 6 June 2008, after three years of incredible resilience and bravery, Mum is gone. Despite everything we'd been through, it's still so devastatingly hard.

We lay her to rest in the Yarra Valley, in among her beloved mountains. The stroke had taken away so much from her, but we were given the blessing of keeping an angel with us on earth for three more precious years.

At her funeral we read her favourite psalm and remember her beautiful life.

We cry, and it helps to bring a little bit of healing to all our broken hearts.

I emerge from the shadows, back on the Great Himalaya trail and catch up to Cal, Bek, Matt and Tsering Lama. They're waiting for me on a rock below in the sun.

I give them a hug and they pull on their backpacks and we continue on. Cal's still feeling slightly nauseous, but he's walking a lot more strongly and I'm confident he'll make it all the way to camp this afternoon.

It takes us several hours, with lots of stops and starts, but we reach the tiny teahouse as the sun sinks in the west and the silhouettes of the mighty peaks stand up to stretch along the skyline.

We set up our little yellow tents on a grassy space in the backyard and watch the yaks come faithfully home along their narrow, well-worn trails. The moon rises in the sky and it spills a silvery lunar light across our campsite. I say goodnight to Cal. He's in the tent next to mine, thankfully he's had some dinner and is feeling much better. Soon he's fast asleep.

I lean out of my little yellow tent, cocooned in my sleeping bag, and look up at the stars in the sky … and think for awhile.

This 1700-kilometre journey that we're on, that's taking us far across the mountains and valleys of Nepal, from soaring highs to plunging lows, is a mirror image of our lives. And just like my mum, this trail is teaching me to treasure those times when the sun is on my face, and to celebrate loved ones, health and life.

Then when it's tough, and the valley is deep, and I feel like yelling out, 'Why?!' I won't give up regardless of whatever happens in this imperfect life of mine. Because just like Mum, I'll find the trail back up to those beloved mountains, and just like her I will find the strength and the determination to go on … and on … and on.

# Chapter Twelve

# TO THE END OF THE TRAIL AND BEYOND

## *The Great Himalaya Trail*

## 2016

Stowed away, in a little green dry sac in the middle of my backpack, are my two well-worn, well-loved, dog-eared diaries. 'Precious cargo', I call them.

They're in here with all the other irreplaceable things in my world right now—TG the Bear, my mum's gold wristwatch and my dad's folded handkerchief—things I've brought all the way from home to balance with me up on the shoulders of nature's most amazing body of work—the Great Himalaya Trail.

So far, I've managed to keep theses diaries safe from all the elements—the snow and the wild winds, from the searing sun, the glacial river crossings, the dust and the drenching monsoonal rains—and every single day, except for that one epic day when we crossed over the high passes of Sherpani Col and West Col, and scraped the sky at 6189 metres, I've opened them up to write. Often I would be huddled in my little yellow tent away from the wind and the cold, and at other times I'd be on a rock, in the afternoon sun, with the Himalayas reading over my shoulders.

I've smudged plenty of words with my sweat and tears and emptied the ink from all of my pens, but I've tried my best to capture in these pages, the magnitude, the majesty, and the profound effect that this incredible trail has had on my life.

Let me unfasten that dry sac, gently open the diary pages and take you back along the trail. Come with me to where my weariness and elation eventually met … to the final days of trekking the Great Himalaya Trail.

## Day 144 – 20 July 2016

*As I write this I have a growing sense of how close we are to the end of our journey.*

*The terrain we're trekking through this afternoon has changed dramatically, from deep ravines filled with raging, muddy torrents, topped up by the rain, to dry, open valleys dotted with villages, dense scrub and dust.*

*Thankfully the monsoonal clouds are hanging back in the east today. They're finally giving up on us and allowing a blue-sky afternoon to burst through.*

*This means we can pack away our rain jackets and recharge our phones and cameras from our portable solar panels on our packs. Their batteries are desperately low.*

*Today my spirits are high.*

*I'm not as tired as I was yesterday, which is good news, because I know my reserves are pretty much running on empty now. Every morning as I get dressed I'm aware of the looseness of* my clothes and that I'm onto my last hole in my belt. I see my tired, thin face in my tiny square mirror. The extreme physical demands of this trail have taken their toll but I wouldn't swap this experience for anything. It's given me back so much.

Only a handful of days to go and I'll be able to rest and recover and reflect on this journey.

We've changed our schedule for the next few days. We're going to add in some extra hours of walking today, and tomorrow, and strategically this will bring us to within striking distance of our finish line, which is the Nepalese border town of Hilsa.

To mark the occasion, we're working on a banner for our final photos. Bek is doing the writing and I'm doing the colouring in. I've promised to stay between the lines and be neat!

The white, silk banner will say 'GHT 2016', in big, bold letters, with our English names and our Nepalese names on either side.

After this trek, Juddha, our guide, will hang it up in the dining room at the World Expeditions permanent campsite, in Dengboche, alongside T-shirts and banners from other mountaineering expeditions. I'd love to see it again one day.

It's surreal to think we're only a few kilometres from Tibet, and so close to closing this chapter of our lives. I've pictured this moment from the very first day when I pulled on my shiny, brown leather trekking boots. Today they're scuffed and the tread is worn and the sole of my left boot is just hanging on.

The sun has slipped away for another day and the coolness of the evening is rising up from the valley. The stars are stepping out across the sky.

I'm going to fall asleep listening to my favourite song, 'Under the Milky Way Tonight' and dream of going home.

## Day 145 – 21 July 2016

*I think the building excitement and anticipation really carried my feet along today.*

*I kept a surprisingly fast pace as I scrambled up the shortcuts between the sweeping switchbacks.*

*Cal and I had an awesome chat about the unbelievable prospect of reaching Hilsa tomorrow, and then turning ourselves for home.*

*What will it be like stepping back into our lives again, after all this time out on the trails alone, with just us and our expedition team, alone with our thoughts, with the mountains, with the sky and the starry heavens above. It will be a culture shock. Will we be ready?*

*What about family, friends, shopping centres, social media and day-to-day life?*

*Will I be confident enough to drive in peak-hour traffic? How will I cope with crowds? Will I remember my pin number for my credit card?*

*How much have I changed and will I fit back in? I don't really know …*

*But what I do know is that I'm looking forward to seeing Doug again. Having longer conversations than the quick static-filled satellite phone chats that we've had along the trail.*

*I'm looking forward to a swim in the Pacific Ocean, and going for a run and sitting on the Coogee Beach headland with a takeaway coffee in my hand and gazing out at the endless blue expanse.*

*This afternoon the sun peeped through the thick canopy of clouds, lighting sections of the landscape like a slow-moving searchlight. We walked close to 20 kilometres today, and pushed past our original scheduled campsite of the tiny village of Yari, with its bright yellow canola crops, and cluster of weathered, wooden houses.*

*We're now camped just below the final pass—Sarpa La.*
*Tomorrow we will cross over it and descend to Hilsa.*

*It feels surreal to be writing these words on this page:*
*'Tomorrow we will complete the Great Himalaya Trail'.*

*It's hard to believe that every single step, over all these months, has collectively brought us to where we are today.*

## Day 146 – 22 July 2016

*What a day!*

*I'll remember this day, every single day, for the rest of my life.*

*Right now the feelings of exhilaration and absolute relief are washing over me. I'm curled up in my sleeping bag, in my little yellow tent and it's 4.45pm. Here's how the day played out …*

*This morning I was up at 4.30am, getting dressed long before our 5am wake-up call of hot, black tea. I couldn't sleep, as my heart was racing.*

*Today would be the day—after five whole months of trekking, we'd reach the border and realise our dream.*

*Our plan was to leave our campsite set up. The kitchen crew, the ponies and their drivers will remain and rest here, while we press on to the Tibetan border with our much-loved lead guide, Juddha Rai, and our two awesome Sherpas, Lakpa Tamang and Lakpa Sherpa. They've shared so much of this epic journey with us, and have become close like family, so it's absolutely fitting that they'll be the ones walking all the way with us to the end.*

*After a quick breakfast of porridge, eggs and potatoes, and a group photo with our fellow intrepid trekkers, Jasmine and Florian, we headed off up the trail to the pass.*

*It was just on 6am.*

*Mist swirled around us, bringing visibility down to about 20 metres. Tiny drops of water settled on our jackets. We followed*

*a graded gravel road and were soon back up above 4000 metres
again. I could feel the effects of the altitude. We were walking fast
and I was back to being breathless again.*

*Bek, Matt, Cal and I stayed together.*

*It was time to have that reflective conversation that
accompanies the end of any profound experience. We took it in
turns to share our highlights from the trail: the turquoise sacred
lakes, the sunrises and sunsets, the high passes, the stars, the
Nepalese trekking team, the 8000-metre peaks, the fossils in
rocks, the silence, the stillness and the sacredness of this place.*

*So many memories ... the epilogue of so many conversations
together out here on the trail, the prologue of so many reasons to
be drawn back here.*

*The winding road brought us all the way up to the prayer flags
on the pass. It was windy up there, gusting from the west, tearing
through the material of the mist. It was our last pass before the
border. An incredible thought—our last pass! I was so excited.*

*From here we caught our very first glimpse of Tibet.*

*The country changed dramatically beyond this point. It was as
if a line had been drawn at the pass. It was bleak, desolate, dry,
and steep, as if life had deserted these mountains entirely and
they'd been forgotten and left.*

*Across the landscape, large pale landslide areas etched stripes
into the slopes. Sections of the road had been swept away and
there was a tiny, yellow grader working carefully to repair them.*

*We followed the winding road as it hugged the mountainside
and listened intently for falling rocks. We walked as fast as we
could for 18 kilometres, down ... down ... down ...*

*Nomadic shepherds balanced their sheep above us on the shale,
and an oncoming truck kicked up a plume of dust.*

*At last we could see into the deep valley below, to the waters*

*of the grey, silty river and to the tiny township of Hilsa.
It seemed such a little place, to be playing such a momentous role
in our lives, with its cluster of ageing buildings, bright blue roofs
and helipad.*

*Next to Hilsa, a metal suspension bridge spanned the river to
the border post. That was our endpoint! We had just one steep
rocky shortcut to go.*

*As I scrambled down the final embankment, the sole on my
left boot came away. It was as if it knew its job was done. It
had hung in there all the way across this amazing country, until
today.*

*I tightened the strap of my gaiter underneath it to try to keep
it in place and climbed carefully over the remaining boulders.*

*At last Bek, Matt, Cal and I reached the final stretch of road
on the outskirts of town, and we walked out from the wilderness
into this little pocket of civilisation.*

*Here we were, four weary trekkers, travellers, pilgrims …
finishing this quest, just as we'd started it, together, as a team, as
a close-knit family.*

*We gathered on the concrete steps of the suspension bridge to
celebrate this profound moment in our lives. Cal and Matt with
their long, bushranger beards. Bek and I with hilarious hat hair.
All many kilograms lighter. All wearing faded T-shirts, carrying
dusty backpacks, and with our belt buckles done up as tightly as
they could go. We may have looked so much better at other times
in our lives, but we'd never been so elated and alive!*

*Juddha Rai, Lakpa Tamang and Lakpa Sherpa gently draped
us in traditional Nepalese silk scarves and we celebrated with
Jasmine and Florian. We took photos with our GHT banner
held high. I looked at the letters—GHT. I hadn't done too bad
a job colouring them in, and even though they were only three
letters, they shouted out about so much.*

*There was now just one more thing to do, to finish this journey off.*

*We all walked across the suspension bridge to the concrete wall of the Tibetan border, to where armed guards stood unflinchingly at their posts.*

*This was the very end of our epic journey west. In among a steady stream of traders and Indian pilgrims passing by, we hugged and laughed and cried.*

*So here I am, nestled in my sleeping bag, back at camp.*

*We have three days to retrace our footsteps back to the town of Simikot, to catch our flight out.*

*For the first time, in a long time tomorrow, we'll be trekking east, facing the rising sun, starting for real on our journey home.*

## Day 152 – 28 July 2016

*It's Day 152 of the Great Himalaya Trail, 152 days since we started in Taplejung, in the east, and our last official day of our incredible trek across Nepal.*

*We've reached Simikot. Our trekking is over. It's time to fly back to Kathmandu.*

*Our red World Expeditions bags are being loaded into the cargo hold as we board our plane and find our seats. Time is of the essence. A fleeting gap has appeared in the swirling morning mist, big enough to squeeze through and start our journey back home. Our plane taxies quickly and races into the sky to beat the incoming mist.*

*Very soon, beneath our wings, all the racing rivers, the switchback trails and those towering mountains, all those things that have become so familiar to us, slip quietly away. It's difficult to believe that after 1700 kilometres of trekking, our GHT journey has finally come to an end.*

*Right now our heads and hearts are brimming with emotion and we fill the cabin with laughter and tears. This trek has been so much more than a scheduled, methodical journey across the countryside—it's been a life-changing experience, and as we set our course for home, I begin to reflect on where our wandering steps have taken us.*

*Nepal is such an incredible country—diverse, rugged and breathtaking—it instantly captured my heart and soul. I have so many favourite places.*

*The far eastern part of Nepal, where all the jagged, snow-capped peaks of the Kanchenjunga region jut skyward between rocky passes and boulder strewn glaciers.*

*In the west, where the thick, green juniper forests grow bravely in steep ravines that gradually give way to high, shaley windswept plateaus.*

*In the Everest region, where the magnificent mountain itself stands shoulder to shoulder with its fellow 8000-metre peaks, and in the Makalu region, where a distant evening thunderstorm flashed on the ice, and the stars were so bright that the Milky Way painted a vibrant white stripe across the inky sky.*

*Dotted throughout this amazing country are tiny little villages. These are the pockets of life found on mountainsides and in valleys, filled with stone houses, terraced crops of maize, and colourful, welcoming teahouses.*

*The children come running when they see us arrive. They're curious and chatty and ask for pens and chocolate and want to know our names. We catch glimpses of daily life as people wash clothes and fill containers at the local communal water tap. Goats and yaks wander with us, along the narrow, dusty streets.*

*The culture and religion here is so incredibly rich. Untouched. Passed carefully down through the generations. I've been swept up in its beauty and reverence. There are stupas, monasteries, and* flapping lines of prayer flags. I've taken so many photos. It's truly wonderful to think that life and faith has remained unchanged here for so many centuries.

Out along the trail the people are welcoming, warm-hearted and kind. I love their expressive faces and colourful clothes. They greet us with 'Namaste', and ask where we're going. They are so surprised when we tell them we're from Australia, and we're walking the length of Nepal—that's a long way from home, they say, and a very long way to go!

They have an amazing resilience, and they're wise beyond words. They've been through a lot, particularly those in the Langtang region, who are piecing their lives back together after the devastating earthquake and landslide. It was with heavy hearts that we walked across the vast area of mud and rock, the place where their village had once stood, but there are encouraging signs and hope as rebuilding takes place across the region.

The Nepalese people are so grateful that trekkers are returning to their trails. They are relieved that we're coming back to buy their produce, to stay in their campsites and teahouses, and employ them as Sherpas, porters and guides. This is life-giving income for them, enabling them to rebuild their homes and lives.

With its changing seasons, challenging altitudes, snow, heat and monsoonal rains, the Great Himalaya Trail has been truly magnificent. It's challenged me to the point of absolute fatigue, given me incredible moments of joy when I've climbed the high passes, and then finally made it to Hilsa, our finishing line on the border of Tibet. This journey has given me the chance to reflect on life, to think about my goals and dreams, and brought me even closer to my amazing children who trekked alongside me the whole way.

Thank you to our Nepalese team—our guardian angels on

*earth, our extended family, our dear friends who have been with
us, watching over us, all the way. We could not have done this
journey without you.*

*Finally, after another connecting flight, our plane touches down
in Kathmandu. We're back among the buildings, the motorbikes
and the late afternoon rush. Horns sound and engines rev and
our bus is swept along with the bustling tide.*

*Out west, beyond the foothills, the sun is sinking; it's an
orange dusty ball. It reminds me of where we've come from today,
from the trail, from the remote and misty plateaus.*

*Now we are far, far away from our little yellow tents that we
knew so well, from the crunch of the snow, and the tall, green
forests and the majestic mountain peaks, far from the serenity and
the skies and the stars.*

*But in my head and heart, I'll hold onto these memories for
the rest of my life, and I know, whenever I need to, I'll close
my eyes and take myself back. Back to the wilds of the Great
Himalaya Trail.*

So now I'll close my diary and put it safely back into its dry
sac. I'm very much aware my time with you is drawing to a
close—this book is almost finished … my journey here is over.

But it's your turn now.

I'd love you to close your eyes and sit quietly for a moment.

Think about your life and friends and loved ones. About
your dreams and the hopes you have in life.

Forget about your battles and the discouragements of the
past and the doubts that may be holding you back.

Be kind to yourself. Trust yourself. Believe in yourself.

Listen to the instincts that bubble up from deep within …

It's time for you to go … go somewhere you've never been before and to do something new.

Follow a passion, act on an adventure, get fitter, sign up for an event, volunteer, raise funds for charity, start a new hobby, a project, travel around your comfort zone, then push your boundaries further out.

But most of all, be brave, live in hope, and everyday—no matter what it may bring, or how you may feel—live your life to the full!

Wear out some trekking boots, fade some T-shirts, get out in your crumpled gardening shorts, cross some finish lines or swim in the sea. You may have looked so much better at other times in your life, but you'll have never felt so elated and alive!

Then if you can, buy yourself a diary and in big bold letters write these two words right next to your name: 'Adventurous Spirit'. Because that's what you are.

Go ahead and fill up the pages with your journeys and dreams. Smudge your words with sweat and tears and empty the ink from all of your pens. Do your best to capture the magnitude, the majesty, and the profound effect that these new experiences are having on your life.

I'll be looking out for you, on the path less travelled, and when I see you, I'll get alongside, I'll encourage you and I'll walk with you all the way to the end.

There we can set up camp. We can watch as the winter sun sits itself squarely on the westerly horizon, not moving much at all, distracted.

We can gaze up at the moon as it coaxes a handful of stubborn stars back into the majestic, deepening blue canopy of the sky, and together we can look heavenwards and know there is always a way through.

H xx

The end ... but not quite yet ...

# EPILOGUE

## 2017

As I reflect back on my running journey, I know that the 2012 Mother's Day Classic was a huge game changer in my life, in so many ways. Back then I had a couple of clear reasons to run, now there are lots!

I run today because I'll never forget how I felt during that very first race, discovering that freedom of flying on my feet and that incredible elation of reaching the finish line.

I run to share the journey with my family and the camaraderie of other race participants.

I run because I love to challenge myself ... to go further ... adding in elements of difficulty like snow, cold, and altitude to increase the adventure of it all. It's about me pushing back at being defined by cancer.

I'm not running away from anything, but towards a goal, something bigger than myself. Not because I'm frightened, but because I'm trying to be brave.

I run so I can remember people and dedicate races to them and carry them with me. And to raise funds for cancer research and to encourage others.

It also gives me precious time alone with my thoughts, so I can process life, plan, pray, dream.

Through all these experiences, life has taught me that we can end up in places that we never really planned to go, and that's okay!

I believe that every new day brings with it an amazing opportunity to stand at a brand-new start line and we can pull on our 'old baggy gardening shorts and our faded stripy T-shirt' in whatever form that may take, and follow our instincts, dare ourselves to dream and simply go ... go ... go ...

... and as for my plans for the future ... I'm so excited to be returning to Nepal to revisit the magnificent Himalayas in October 2017, on a trek to raise funds for cancer research. I'll get to see the mountains again and our GHT banner hanging in the Dengboche teahouse.

Then I'll be running the Volcano Marathon in the Atacama Desert in Chile in November 2017 ...

And after that? Well, I guess we'll just have to see!

# ACKNOWLEDGEMENTS

To Mum and Dad, and my brothers, Trevor and Ray, I am blessed beyond measure to have travelled life's journey with you. You are more precious than all the stars in heaven.

My dearest husband, Doug, I love you to bits. I'm in one piece today because of your love and support. It was you who encouraged me to swim out into the ocean waves, to find my legs to run and to open up my wings to fly.

To my daughter and son, Bek and Cal, for your awesome love and companionship. Thank you for being there every single step of the way along the Great Himalaya Trail. You are the next generation of adventurous spirits and I know we're in good hands! (To Matt, too—welcome to our family.)

To Dr Christopher Bradbury and Professor Michael Friedlander, thank you for saving my life.

To my publisher, Lou Johnson, for your beautiful support and the belief that the story I carried within was worthy to be mapped out in words and for trusting me with the task!

To my editorial and design team: Michele Perry, Kit Carstairs, Jane Price and Vivian Valk—your guidance and care has been absolutely brilliant. What a journey together—you've really brought my book, my story, to life!

For the cover photography, thanks goes to my husband for taking such a precious family photo, to Mark Conlon for capturing my elated post-race face at the North Pole Marathon, and to Douglas Frost for such a fantastic action shot at my beloved Coogee Beach.

The Severin family at Curtin Springs Cattle Station, you welcomed me into your family as one of your own. Thank you for an unforgettable year in the red dust.

To the Coogee Surf Lifesaving Club for training me to be a surf lifesaver and creating a remarkable seaside community in the middle of Australia's biggest city.

Rob de Castella, thank you for your incredible inspiration and friendship.

Richard Donovan, for your unrivalled vision in creating the North Pole Marathon and the World Marathon Challenge. You lead the way—inspiring, life-changing stuff.

To my fellow marathoners at the North Pole and the World Marathon Challenge, your friendship will last a lifetime. I'd run with you all again anytime, anywhere! Just let me know when and I'll pull on my runners.

World Expeditions for your life transforming treks—the Great Himalaya Trail is a journey like no other.

To our dear Nepali family of guides, Sherpas, cooks and porters, I look forward to sharing the trails with you again. You are true guardian angels and teachers of what's really important in life.

To The Salvation Army for being an amazing Christian organisation that saves lives in more ways than one. Yours is a faith in action, and a love with its sleeves rolled up.

To the Can Too Foundation for the opportunity to be an ambassador and to raise funds for cancer research. I love the difference you are making in people's lives.

ANZGOG (Australia New Zealand Gynaecological Oncology Group) for the groundbreaking medical care you provide for women with gynaecological cancers.

Ovarian Cancer Australia for your incredible support for women with ovarian cancer.

To all my friends, young and old, near and far, from childhood to the present—my life is far richer for knowing you.

And thank you, dear reader, for joining me on this journey.

Here's to more adventures together!

Hugs, H xx